About th

Christopher Spencer, (not his real name), has worked in the banking and construction sectors and as an Adviser to Government. He has over 50 years of experience in international business and finance and has qualifications in economics, accountancy, and banking. He is still active in business and now works on promoting new "Green" technologies.

Christopher lives in London with his wife and has two grown-up children. He also has several grandchildren. He likes solitary walks and reading about international politics and world history. But he also reads modern poetry and detective stories. In 2021, Christopher Spencer published his first book "Manna from Heaven and other True Stories." His first book has received 5-Star reviews.

Praise for "Manna from Heaven and other True Stories" by the same author.

"Amazing and true insights into a fascinating life on the dark side of international business and politics."

"It really is like reading about James Bond's Accountant and I could not recommend this book more."

"A good insight into government and international business."

To my grandchildren, with love.

The Sound of Guns and Other True Stories

The Truth Is Too Often Stranger Than Fiction

To Bob,
With My Very Best Wishes,
Christopher Spencer.

CHRISTOPHER SPENCER

Copyright © 2023 by Christopher Spencer.
This edition published in 2023.

All rights reserved. No part of this publication may be reproduced, stored in any form of retrieval system or transmitted in any form or by any means without prior permission in writing from the publishers except for the use of brief quotations in a book review.

The moral rights of the author have been asserted for this work in accordance with the Copyright, Designs and Patents Act 1988.

ISBNs:
978-1-80541-305-9 (paperback)
978-1-80541-306-6 (eBook)

Published in 2023 by Publishing Push Ltd.,
30 Stamford St., London SE1 9LQ.

Contents

Preface to Shorter True Stories vii
The Sound of Guns 1
Wall Street and Beyond... 21
The Battle... 41
Another Country 51
Sea Dreams 73
Fine Weather and a Fair Wind 89
The New Man..111
The Cause 137
By The Lakes..157
The Warrior 183
Speed Boats.. 213
A Bridge Too Far... 227
The Time Machine...251
Hot Lips... 265
The King of Italy... 289
Irish Mist 317
Acknowledgements 345

"Difficulties are meant to rouse not discourage. The human spirit is to grow stronger by conflict."
— ***William Ellery Channing***

"It is not the strongest of the species that survives, not the most intelligent that survives. It is the one that is the most adaptable to change."
— ***Charles Darwin***

PREFACE TO SHORTER TRUE STORIES

"I write because there is a voice within me that will not be still." – Sylvia Plath.

In the preface to his Ashenden stories, William Somerset Maugham candidly noted that "Fact is a poor story teller." These tales, spun from his personal experiences as a spy in Switzerland during the First World War, resonated with me. Similarly, my first foray into storytelling yielded seven true novelettes collectively titled "Manna from Heaven and other True Stories."

All of those stories were autobiographical and sprang from my experience of fifty years in international finance and business. Most of them showed the intrigue, corruption, and conspiracy that are prevalent in that world and remains so to this day. Two of my true stories were firmly placed in the field of espionage. To separate out my autobiographical writing from my continuing working life in business, I wrote them under the nom de plume of "Christopher Spencer", which, I must apologise, I still intend to use.

I found that I was hampered by always trying to tell the truth, and trying to weave the truth into a story can indeed, as Maugham observed, be very difficult. But the truth is often highly inconvenient, and therefore it needs to be told. However, the truth is also too often stranger than fiction and therefore should make much more interesting reading. That is provided, of course, that the reader remembers that the author is limited in what he can write by the nature of reality, as well as by what he has actually experienced.

Unfortunately, we now live in a culture of induced consumer greed and what has been called a "Post-Truth Society." Too often these days, I believe, many people live in "Bubbles of Unreality" and it is often very difficult for them to separate out what is the truth from pure fiction, or from the repeated lies promulgated by politicians and the social and mass media. It is perhaps, therefore, useful to show them a little of what, unfortunately, goes on in the "Real World".

Because all of my stories are substantially true, I have had to change people's names in most cases, but I do not change the places or the circumstances. In one of my novelettes, I did not name the country involved as the venal man that my story was about was still the Head of State there, as I wrote it. He is now on trial for corruption.

I sometimes take certain literary licence with the sequence of events, passing from the present into the past, and sometimes,

PREFACE TO SHORTER TRUE STORIES

into the future. But this is to try and provide a more interesting and entertaining experience for my readers. Where I have used some short quotes from published works, I acknowledge and give thanks to the authors, or if they are dead, to their estates.

Now I am embarking on a series of Shorter True Stories; they are shorter than my seven novelettes but are still equally as true. Some of them are about events in my long business career, whilst others are much more personal, relating to my young adulthood, or childhood. In the latter case, they are glimpses into a lost world. It really is "The Land of Lost Content" of A.E. Housman, as I was born in the beautiful county of Shropshire and am therefore a true "Shropshire Lad." As well as England, the other country that I had a lot to do with when I was younger, was Wales. My maternal grandmother moved there in the circumstances set out in one of my stories and, as a boy, I used to visit her where she then lived, in a wild and glorious place.

One of the true short stories is not by me; it is a narrative written by my grandmother's lover, of a great naval battle in which he took part during the First World War. I have merely added a Foreword. Another story is set some nine years before I was born and is about the true events that occurred during my parent's honeymoon. A further story concerns more recent events which, although told to me by another, I have reason to believe is true.

I will, no doubt, be accused of nostalgia to which I would plead "Guilty as Charged!" Only our Past is certain. The Present is but a second's Dream. Our Future is still totally unknown.

I was brought up as an only child, and a left-handed one at that. As I refused to write with my other hand, I was eventually expelled from my first fee-paying school. Fortunately, I had no competition from siblings for my parent's attention. I found it difficult to make friends and I loved my own company. I still like long, solitary walks, during which I can think, and increasingly, talk to myself! But short stories are not an easy genre to write; one must always remember to limit them in length, but make sure that they still contain sufficient detail to be self-contained and entertain the reader. In my case, I also have to make them true to what I have actually experienced.

I have mixed these stories up; they are not in any particular time sequence as perhaps my seven Novellas, in some ways, were. But I have kept the stories about my childhood and early adult life in a sequence, so that my readers can begin to understand my earlier history. Just two of the stories take place before I was even born but are based upon true facts.

Then the sequence moves to my childhood and the interruption of my settled, comfortable life, caused by my father's addiction to gambling. This led to an eventual family breakdown and years of abject poverty. Having completed my interrupted schooldays, the sequence then moves on to my first job, and from there to my politically turbulent university years as a mature student. In the interests of truth, I have even included a very personal story of one of my failed love affairs.

The rest of these Shorter True Stories have occurred during my long and varied international career. I have always found that the Truth is almost always much stranger than Fiction. Ian Fleming, the creator of the now famous British agent James Bond, worked in British Naval Intelligence during the Second World War and then used that experience to write his fictional stories. After that war, he became a journalist, and in 1959 and 1960, he was sent by his newspaper around the world to visit certain cities in Asia, North America, and Europe. The result was a book about his experiences called "Thrilling Cities" published in 1962.

In the Author's Note, at the beginning of that book, Fleming wrote something that I thought was apposite with my stories too. While calling his true accounts of the various cities he visited "Mood Pieces," Fleming writes that "such information as they provide is focussed on the bizarre and perhaps the shadier side of life." I recognised immediately that this was also true about a lot of my stories, based upon my own experiences. I do not apologise for that. I cannot because my stories are not fiction; they are all true.

Sometimes I feel that my main character Edwards, which is me, is like one of the hapless, accidental "heroes" of some of the stories of Eric Ambler, who find themselves caught up in complex, difficult, and even dangerous situations not of their own making. Ambler was one of the greatest writers of fictional thrillers of his time, and indeed served as an inspiration for Ian Fleming.

But, I am not a hero; indeed, I am very much a coward! Although my stories are non-fiction, in some of them I have had to use a little artistic licence to give some background to the facts that I know, or have been told.

When I write about my childhood, I do not use the name Edwards, but just write about "the boy" who once was me. I have also written, as truthfully as I can, about my parents and my grandparents. This can perhaps be the most painful, personal thing to do. Parent's actions can, so easily, set the future for their children and for their children's children.

But, as one gets older, one can see your parents more clearly, as the flawed human beings that they once were, and indeed,

PREFACE TO SHORTER TRUE STORIES

that all of us are. Then one can hopefully start to forgive them for their defects and learn something of the real and usually deeply hidden reasons for their actions. After all, I have to try to understand and sympathise with them, for I also have some terrible defects myself!

The title of this book, "The Sound of Guns," is taken from a quote attributed to the first Baron Rothschild, and my true stories include some that are about war, or the circumstances of military action. Life, like war, is a struggle for a continuing existence; it is fought against disease, violence, hunger, and ignorance. It is, in the words of the great Charles Darwin about "the Survival of the Fittest". This is necessary for the human race to evolve further.

But so it must be if we are to maintain human progress. As we are now finding in the 21st century, there is a limit to what the State can do for its people. But this is also an era of a belief in "entitlement;" a dangerous claim that takes away from morality, and from what it is to be human.

Respect must always be earned through people's actions, and a good living obtained by study and hard work. Those that feel "entitled" to these things and fail to achieve them, become bitter, blame others for their own inadequacies, and then try to divide society further. Others descend into defeat, despair, and drug and alcohol abuse.

Human beings can never be equal; if it is not background, it is character, health, or intelligence that defines us. But those that really fail must still be protected; in 1875 Karl Marx summarised it so well: "From each according to their ability, to each according to their needs".

However, we must also always remember the need for historic continuity as we are all "Flames of Consciousness". We are lit, we burn for a while, and then we are extinguished. But, while we burn, we can illuminate and try and understand the World in which we somehow find ourselves, as well as the vast Universe, of which our World is such a tiny part. We must also try to pass on our experiences to the next generations in an effort to try to teach and help them to avoid having to learn from the same mistakes that we made! That is what I have, very modestly, in my own way, tried to do.

– Christopher Spencer.
London. August 2022.

THE SOUND OF GUNS

"When you hear the Sound of Guns, Buy!" attributed to Nathaniel, the 1st Baron Rothschild.

1

Edwards sat at his desk at one end of the long, open-planned office. There were about a dozen desks in the large room. Behind him sat his Manager, and in front of him, at another desk which was pushed close to his, sat the son of the Chieftain of a leading Scottish Clan. His close colleague was modest and charming; he had attended a leading Public School which had been founded in the reign of Queen Elizabeth the First and was located in what had now become a leafy suburb of Northwest London. Whenever he could, this man tried to visit his parents who lived in a castle set in the glorious wilds of Scotland.

Edwards had answered his colleague's telephone on several occasions, whilst he was absent from his desk, discovering how well connected he was in the process. One voice, who had asked to speak to him numerous times, was unmistakable. It was the Heir to the Throne. But he had not identified himself, and Edwards had pretended not to recognise who it was on the other end of the line. Edwards had asked if he had wanted to leave a message, but "No. I will call him back later," was all that the Prince of Wales would say.

It was now the latter half of the 1970's and Edwards was working for an illustrious merchant bank in the City of London founded by a leading German family in the 19th century. He had already been working in the financial centre of the City of London for over five years, first for another Merchant Bank, and then for a leading Stockbroking firm. He had been introduced to this bank by a university friend who worked in the department of the bank that dealt with German business. Before coming to England, his friend had been raised in Germany solely by his mother, as his father had been killed on the Eastern Front, while serving as an officer in the German Wehrmacht, during the Second World War.

Of those that were British, in the big office in which Edwards now sat, only Edwards and his Manager were without some kind of title. Behind Edwards's right shoulder sat a Lord, who owned one of the finest grand Jacobean stately homes in England. Down the room were a collection of mere "Honourables," both men and women. Only Edwards and his Manager had not benefited from an expensive private school education, and they were only there because the bank had changed its recruitment policy a few years before. Previously, they had only recruited for senior posts from people who had attended a top Public School and then had graduated from one of the two leading British Universities.

Edwards could offer neither; he had simply been an only child, albeit a bright one, who had somehow found his way into a good Grammar School. But then disaster had struck: his father's addiction to gambling had resulted in the breakup of the family, leading to years of poverty for him and his mother. Edwards had then joined a major commercial bank as soon as he was old enough to do so. He had studied hard in the evenings, and during any spare time that he had from working in various branches of this bank and as a result had managed to pass all his banking examinations at a relatively early age. After that he had decided to apply to take an economics degree at one of the colleges of London University.

Edwards' first few years at his present bank had been concerned with working on their British banking business, where he found his Director to be a stickler for detail and correctness. When applications for a customer to be given a loan were put together, to be considered by the bank's Credit Committee, Edwards had to research and write them up. Time and again they were returned by his Director, who was not satisfied with what Edwards had produced. But Edwards did not mind; he recognised that this man had a brilliant analytical mind. He could forensically analyse a set of company accounts, and look behind the figures, into the real operations of the company. Edwards recognised that he could learn a lot from him.

At Christmas time, each staff member received a large Harrods Hamper and an invitation for themselves and their wife, or husband, to attend the Christmas Party. This was always held at a leading London hotel where they were received by the bank's Chairman, a Scottish Peer who would go on to hold the most senior position in the Royal Household. Also present was a direct descendant of the German founders: a man who still owned a large part of the bank's shares and was one of the richest men in Britain. As well as his land, houses, and money, this man owned a unique collection of precious objects.

One day Edwards had the opportunity to visit the Strong Room of the bank, which was hidden down in the deepest basement of the building. There he was fortunate enough to be shown some of these artefacts by the Curator who was charged with looking after them. Among them was a glorious, antique orrery of the Earth, showing also the Moon and the Planets. It was some five feet high, made from solid gold, and covered with precious jewels. "There are only three of these in the World," said the Curator, "and two of those are in leading Museums."

"How much might it be worth, do you think?" asked Edwards naively.

The Curator smiled at him. "In an auction," he replied, "the bidding would start at over two million pounds!"

But the man who owned all this appeared to be of doubtful ability, as far as business was concerned. Although he owned the majority of the bank, Edwards had heard rumours of how the other Directors of the bank carefully scrutinised everything that he tried to do.

2

One morning whilst sitting at his desk, Edwards saw his colleague who sat opposite him, approach their Manager. Although they spoke in low voices, Edwards could hear clearly what was being said behind him.

"Do you mind if I take off an extra hour for lunch today please?" asked Edwards's colleague.

"Of course not," replied their Manager. "Are you going somewhere nice for lunch?"

Lowering his voice even further, hoping that nobody else could hear, Edwards's modest colleague replied: "Actually, I am going to Buckingham Palace for a private lunch with the Queen."

There was a long pause. "Take as long as you like," said their Manager.

When he returned from his long lunch, Edwards looked at his colleague. "I heard you say where you were going," he said. "How did it go?"

"It was lovely," was the reply. "She was so kind to me. She asked me to sit next to her and talked to me all through the meal. Charles and Anne were there too so there were only the four of us at the lunch."

Sometime later, when a new female graduate had joined the bank, she had been assigned a desk in the open-plan room too, a little further down from Edwards. He made it his business to welcome her and realised straight away that she must have attended a leading girls' Public School. She had then gone on to read so-called "Modern Greats," or "Philosophy, Politics, and Economics" at Oxford University. One morning, Edwards saw that her desk was covered with piles of ancient looking documents; intrigued, he made a point of passing her desk and then stopped.

"Whatever are all those?" he asked her.

"They are the deeds to a piece of land that my family has just bought," she answered. "They want a loan, from this bank, against a mortgage on this land. I have been given the task of sorting out all of these in the correct order. I really do not know where to begin!"

Edwards took pity on her. He knew about the requirements for determining a "chain of title," or ownership of a piece of land, from his studies of law during his banking examinations. During his days in commercial banking, he had often established a "title to land" as part of taking a mortgage for one of his branch's customers. He offered to help and, by the end of the day, he had placed all the documents, many of them hundreds of years old, into the right chronological order, thereby establishing a clear line of ownership. Then he made a list of all the documents, now properly ordered, to present to his then employer.

The young Lady, for that was her title as the daughter of a noble family, was suitably grateful. A few days later, she presented Edwards with a small present.

"You were so kind to help me, I want to give you these," she said. "They have been in my family for years. Maybe you can keep them, and one day they may be valuable."

She handed Edwards a number of printed certificates: Imperial Russian Railway bearer bonds that were printed in Russian, French, and English, and issued during the reign of the last Russian Tsar. Her family had subscribed to this bond issue to finance some of the railway lines being constructed within Russia, during the last years of the nineteenth century. After the Russian Revolution of 1917, they had become worthless. But, Edwards was grateful for this kind gesture, and pleased that he had been able to use his knowledge to help her. He had the bonds framed, and placed around the walls of the room that he used as his office at home.

After a couple of years at this bank, Edwards was called in to see the Senior Banking Director. He was a friendly and encouraging individual, already close to retirement. It was he that had first interviewed Edwards, and offered him a job at the bank. "We have decided to give you a change of scene," he said smiling. "You will still sit at the same desk, but you will now be in charge of our small, but growing, portfolio of Middle Eastern business."

Edwards asked a few questions that he thought were pertinent.

"You will be reporting to a new Director," said the Senior Director. He then named the man who owned most of the bank!

"When do I start?" asked Edwards.

"In one month's time," was the reply. "Meanwhile, try and learn as much as you can about your future task."

So Edwards went out and bought himself some books about the Middle East and, to help him understand the Arab Culture, some books about Islam as well. In his spare moments or, when he was travelling on the long Tube train journey from home to work and back, he read voraciously. He studied the small portfolio of existing Middle Eastern business that the bank already had and noted that a large part of it was in Saudi Arabia. So, he bought himself an excellent book on the history of the Saudi Kingdom, and began reading that too. Fortunately, he found that he could absorb the new knowledge quickly.

One day, he was called up to the top Executive Floor to meet the new Director to whom he would now report. Edwards paused along the corridor to this man's office; the walls were hung with a great collection of original works by Marc Chagall who was obviously the favourite artist of the man that he was about to meet. Chagall, who had synthesised the art forms of Cubism,

Symbolism, and Fauvism, and had given rise to Surrealism, certainly suited this man!

Although immensely wealthy, and from a family that had produced many bankers, he appeared to be little interested in banking. He had an edgy personality, his mind darting quickly from one subject to another. He asked some unusual questions, which Edwards tried to answer truthfully while trying to make clear that he was still learning about the Middle East, and doing business there.

"No matter," came the reply. "You must meet the two ------ ------ brothers." Edwards remembered quickly that these two brothers from Lebanon were now closely associated with his bank and had once established a small bank of their own in their native country. They had moved to London when, during one of the civil wars in their unfortunate country, an artillery shell had come through the wall of their bank's offices in Beirut!

3

As soon as he thought that he had learnt enough about Middle Eastern matters, Edwards arranged to meet the two Lebanese brothers. They had a small suite of offices on one of the top floors of the building, which they used from time to time. Edwards found them both to be educated, experienced, and charming. He began to feel that, working closely with them, he might be able to achieve something. The only problem was that they both travelled extensively and were really only in London for a small portion of their time. Therefore, his new job would also have to be about managing them while they were both on the move, and usually at a great distance. After their meeting, he mused on the problems that this situation could produce.

The following morning, he received a telephone call; it was the Secretary to the Vice Chairman of the bank, requesting that he attend a meeting with him that very afternoon. Again he found himself on his way to the top Executive Floor. He had only met the Vice Chairman twice at the annual Christmas Party, but he knew the man's reputation. Although he was a German, he had settled well in the City of London and was very well thought of both in the bank and outside. He was shown into this man's presence, and sat down in front of his large, antique desk.

"I hear that you will now be working for the owner," said the Vice-Chairman, then naming the Director to whom Edwards was now due to report. Edwards agreed that indeed he was and that he was trying to learn as much about the Middle East, and the bank's business there, as quickly as he possibly could.

The Vice Chairman smiled at him and used Edwards's Christian name. "You will understand," he said slowly, "that some of us on the Board are concerned, just a little, about the actions of your new Director. I would like you to make an appointment to see me, every month, and come and tell me in confidence, exactly what he has asked you to do!"

Edwards thought quickly. He was sitting opposite the Vice Chairman of the bank. His new Director was just that, a mere Director, although he owned most of the bank.

"I think that I can do that," he replied.

So there it was! The Board of Directors of his bank did not trust the majority owner of the bank to act sensibly. Poor Edwards was to be in the unenviable position of having to covertly report to the Vice Chairman monthly, on his assignments from the Director to whom he had to report to on a daily basis. It was a very difficult position to be in, and required a level of deviousness on Edwards's part. After the meeting, Edwards sat at his own desk and thought about what he had just been asked to do. In reality, he had been asked to spy on, and then inform on, the bank's main owner.

He did not like doing this; in his university days he had one day been asked by his tutor, who was both an academic and a Government adviser, if he would inform him about the more extreme activities of some of his more radicalised, Marxist or Communist inclined, fellow students. Edwards had not taken up this request. He had thought about it but, somehow, it had seemed unethical to him to do this task. That had been about what were mostly harmless student politics, but this was a much more serious matter. He was employed by this bank and therefore under an obligation to its Directors; it was an entirely different situation.

At last he came to a decision. "So be it," he thought. "I know, at least, where the other Directors are coming from. I will try and work fairly with both parties." But this was a difficult task to contemplate, along with the need to get to know quickly, a region of the World that was completely unknown to him. Behind his desk he squared his shoulders. "I will have a go at doing it," he thought to himself. "After all, it is my career at stake here, and I will have to make the best of this very difficult job that I have now been given."

There was some compensation though: there was a major Conference on the Arab World to be held in Montreux in Switzerland. Edwards was asked to attend, but merely to look after the small stall that his bank would have in the basement of the Palais du Congress for the duration of the Conference. Being recently married, Edwards had asked if he could take his wife. He knew that the Directors, some of whom would also be attending, were taking their wives. Grudgingly this was accepted, as long as he paid for her air fare. Their double room was in only a Three Star hotel, but it would be paid for by the company.

While he worked in the basement of the Palais du Congress, away from daylight, his wife went off every day with the other wives on several interesting trips to see the sights of Switzerland. Only in the evening did he see her, when they had dinner together and then went for a walk along the fashionable Promenade of Montreux. They took in the sights of the sparkling lake and the still snow-capped mountains behind it. They had stayed on for the weekend at their own expense and paid a romantic visit to the lakeside Chateau of Chillon. This had been made famous by Lord Byron, in his poem of 1816, about the imprisonment there of the monk François Bonivard.

4

By now Edwards had learnt quite an amount about the countries of the Middle East, its history, and the Muslim faith which originated there. He knew about the history of Islam and how there were two main types of Muslims. The vast majority of Muslims were Sunnis, but some ten per cent of Muslims were of the Shia denomination. The latter had originated in an early schism, over an argument about who should inherit the title of the Caliph and whether this title should only pass to direct descendants of the Prophet Muhammad.

This schism deepened further after the Battle of Karbala in the late Seventh Century. Edwards drew a parallel between this situation and the historical schism within Christianity, which arose with the emergence of Protestantism. This new movement, which was a "protest" against the power of the Catholic Church and the Pope in Rome, originated in Northern Europe during the sixteenth century. It led to the Hundred Years War and various other conflicts between, these now, two separate sects.

Now Iran was almost exclusively Shia, and there were Shia majorities in Iraq and Bahrain, but these two countries were currently ruled over by a minority Sunni regime. Saudi Arabia had a Shia minority, located mainly in the Eastern Province of that country, but it was the leading Sunni majority country in the region. The Western Powers had not helped; after the First World War and the dissolution of the Ottoman Empire, the British and French Governments had got together to divide the Middle East between them.

The so-called Sykes-Picot Agreement, named after the two civil servants who had drafted it, had drawn many straight lines on the map of the Middle East, irrespective of tribal or religious boundaries. While the Ottomans had divided Iraq into three separate countries for the Shia, the Sunnis, and the Kurds, the Western Powers had united all three into the new country called Iraq and appointed a King to rule over it. Not surprisingly, this had proved to be a recipe for continuing instability.

The Iraqi King had been deposed in 1958 and eventually a new "strong man" called Saddam Hussein had taken over Iraq. With the support of the Americans, he had started a war with Iran in 1980 which had lasted for eight years. Indeed, it had seemed as if the Americans had encouraged him to start this war against the new Fundamentalist Shia Government of Iran, which had deposed the rule of the Shah or King of Iran, a close American ally.

In the 1970's, telephone communication with the Middle East was imperfect and, at one point, Edwards has spent several days in trying to telephone one of the bank's Saudi clients, of which there were a few. This client was a merchant in the port of Jeddah, on the Red Sea. On his behalf, the bank had arranged for a Letter of Credit to be opened to pay for some goods that he wanted to import into Saudi Arabia. But, when the goods had already been dispatched, on a ship bound for Jeddah, the bank had received evidence that they were faulty. Edwards was given the task of contacting this client to tell him this fact.

After days of trying, he eventually managed to make contact and speak to the Saudi merchant directly. To be sure that he understood, Edwards repeated the bad news to him several times, but he need not have worried; the man spoke good English and he appeared to be fully in charge of the situation.

"Do not worry, Mr. Edwards," he had replied. "I will make sure that I examine these goods very carefully first, before arranging for any collection and payment. If I am not happy, I will just refuse delivery and leave the goods in the docks for the seller to collect and transport back, at their own expense."

Edwards continued with his difficult and devious task of keeping his new Director under surveillance but, as well as the pricks of his conscience, he soon began to realise that he was putting himself at risk. There was always the worry that the owner of the bank could find out what he was really doing, or the Vice-Chairman and his other Directors had to take some action to stop the owner carrying out a certain transaction. Then Edwards's duplicitous role in this ongoing situation could become obvious. If this happened, where would he stand? He was a relatively junior member of staff and, no doubt, there was a danger that he could be blamed for what had happened. His lower-class background meant that, unfortunately, he would probably be expendable!

Edwards decided that although his present job was a comfortable one and the company of his civilised colleagues was very pleasant, he would have to consider, in the medium-term, finding some other kind of employment. This he eventually did, leaving the City of London to join a major international construction group, at an attractive salary, to advise them on all matters financial. His new task was also to find the finance for the major projects that they wanted to build, both at home, and abroad.

There was one further telephone call to Saudi Arabia that stood out in Edwards's memory. It was to a British manager who worked for a Saudi company in the city of Dammam, on the shores of the Arabian Gulf. Dammam was the capital of the Eastern Province, which had a large Shia population. The Eastern Province was vital to Saudi Arabia because deep beneath it were most of the oil and gas deposits belonging to the Saudi Kingdom. Edwards at last managed to make telephone contact; it was a good line and he had a long conversation. The only problem was that he could hear an unusually loud noise in the background, about every thirty seconds, during the call.

Edwards struck up a good rapport with his fellow countryman and, as they were finishing their conversation, he decided to ask him a question.

"What is that strange noise in the background that I can hear every half-minute or so?" he asked.

There was a pause, then the other Englishman, sitting in the heat and high humidity of the Arabian Gulf, calmly replied. "That is the Saudi Army. They are using their artillery today to shell the Shia villages that surround the outskirts of this city!"

For the first time Edwards began to understand the bitter dispute between the two sects of Islam. It had taken Christianity several hundreds of years to start to heal the breach between its two factions. It seemed that the breach between the two sects of Islam was even more serious, violent, and long standing, than even Edwards had understood.

Needless to say, there were no reports in the British newspapers, or on radio or television, of what was going on in the Eastern Province of Saudi Arabia. Edwards thought that the British media somehow had a way of ignoring items that might be detrimental to Britain's interests. In the 1970's, Saudi Arabia had turned to Britain for the purchase of the military equipment, of all types, that it needed. This was because of the increasing pro-Israeli sentiment in the United States Congress.

Saudi Arabia had already bought fighter aircraft from Britain in the 1960's, but this business continued to grow, with the purchase of other types of military equipment during the 1970's. It was therefore no surprise that reports that might be critical of the Government of Saudi Arabia, were never reported in Britain.

In 1985, the Kingdom of Saudi Arabia signed the so-called Al Yamamah contract with Britain to provide more fighter aircraft, trainer aircraft, naval vessels, radar systems, missiles, spares, and a range of other weapons for both the Royal Saudi Air Force, and the other Saudi Armed Forces. This contract became the largest single export contract that Britain had ever signed and it is estimated, over the years, to have reached a final total of some Forty-Eight Billion Pounds. The Sound of Guns could certainly prove to be a very profitable business!

WALL STREET AND BEYOND

"When the best paid person in my Bank, is paid more than twenty times the amount of the lowest paid person, then trouble will really start!" attributed to John Pierpont Morgan, Junior and as quoted in the 1930's.

1

It was April, 1984. Edwards and his two colleagues stared up at the great height of the building, in Lower Manhattan, that they were just about to enter. They had flown from London to New York the previous day and had arrived in time for dinner, at their downtown hotel. Over the meal, they had planned what they would say at the meetings that they were scheduled to have over the next few days. Their visit had been set up to meet, first, with several of the major banks in New York, and then to fly on to Washington where they would stay for another couple of nights. Their plan while in Washington was to have meetings there with the World Bank and several of its operating subsidiaries.

All three of them worked for, what was then, Britain's largest construction group. It was felt by the Group's Directors that a visit to America was called for to explore the possibility of financing, from there, some of the projects that they wanted to build around the world. Edwards had been recruited from a merchant bank in the City of London some years before, to advise the group on obtaining finance for such projects, and on other general financial matters. He had asked for two of his colleagues to accompany him as they both played a vital role in the marketing efforts of some of the group's subsidiary companies.

Edwards liked New York, it was vibrant and multi-cultural. His first visit to the city had been as a student, and then he had had to endure the cheap, but doubtful, rather derelict joys of the Times Square Motor Hotel. More recently, he had visited New York with his wife for a holiday. They had stayed with a former business colleague of Edwards and his wife, in their plush New Jersey apartment. From their balcony, the night views over the Hudson River and Manhattan had been stunning. Each morning, the husband had driven Edwards and his wife over the George Washington Bridge and left them in downtown Manhattan, close to Wall Street, where he worked. They were then free to explore the city in their own time, until he collected them, back near Wall Street, in the early evening.

Edwards had always felt that there was an "electric atmosphere" in this city; all things were possible, if you worked hard enough.

Within the great canyons, created by the massive buildings, the inhabitants were always purposeful and went about their business with a great seriousness. The only other city that he had visited that had a similar feeling for him, was the still British colony of Hong Kong.

That first morning, they had visited the New York offices of two leading American banks. They now faced an invitation to lunch at the leading New York bank of J.P. Morgan. This bank had been founded in 1871 by John Pierpont Morgan, Senior, as Drexel, Morgan & Company. However, after the death of Anthony Drexel, the firm was rechristened as J.P. Morgan and Company in 1895. By 1900, it was considered to be one of the most powerful banking houses in the world.

The son of the founder, J.P. Morgan, Junior, took over after the death of his father, and then expanded the bank's business into steel, shipping, and other areas of activity. Although he had some business failures, the bank had become the most prominent bank on Wall Street by the 1930's. Even in the 1980's, it was still considered to be, perhaps, the premier bank headquartered in New York City.

Edwards had been taught well by his Director, in the last merchant bank that he had worked in, to always do his research properly before any meeting with a company took place. This man had also taught him to minutely examine the annual published Report and Accounts of any company, or bank, and to forensically interpret them in the correct way.

Prior to his visit to New York, Edwards had obtained the latest published Report and Accounts of J.P. Morgan from their London branch and had carefully studied them. In them, he had found the photograph of each Board member, and he had identified the Senior Director that they were about to have lunch with, and read his background, which was also included. This man had worked all his life in Wall Street institutions. After he had joined J.P. Morgan, some years before, he had rose rapidly to his current position.

Edwards remembered the famous statement made by J. P. Morgan, Junior in the 1930's, that if ever the highest-paid person in his bank was paid more than twenty times the salary of the lowest paid employee, then trouble would really start. Fortunately, in accordance with American accountancy practices, there was a table in the Report giving the current salaries and bonuses of the bank's current Directors. Edwards worked out that, with the average New York salary, these Directors must now be earning over two hundred times the salary of their more poorly paid colleagues!

How quickly the principles of their founding family had been forgotten in the rampant, avaricious capitalism of the New York City of today! Indeed, the future would soon show the result of setting aside these sensible principles, in a series of financial crises of the late 20th and early 21st centuries. The taxpayer would then be forced to "bail-out" these now poorly managed financial institutions who had undertaken irresponsible, short-term, business opportunities, just to make money, and irrespective of the large risks.

2

The three Englishmen entered the great double doors into the huge, marble reception area; they approached the desk and registered their names, along with the name of their American host. They were asked to take a seat, and told that somebody would soon be sent down from the Executive Floor to collect them. Seated on the comfortable sofa, they compared notes about their meetings that morning, and rehearsed again what they were going to ask this bank, over the luncheon meeting. Their "Jet Lag" was beginning to catch up with them. "I am really looking forward to a good lunch," said Edwards.

He was entertained very regularly in the City of London; banks, insurance brokers, and other financial institutions, were always interested to meet with him to discuss the potential business that they might gain from his large and active employer. He was used to a relaxed atmosphere over a good lunch, with a plentiful supply of wine with the meal and, usually, a round of drinks before the food arrived. For his part, he was often involved in entertaining senior civil servants from various departments of the British government, from whom he was seeking help and even financial support for the various projects that his employer wanted to build around the world.

When travelling, and in an increasingly uncertain world, Edwards always believed that you should eat when you could as you never knew when your next meal might come. Food also helped to keep his mind active and, without it, he found that he could begin to lose energy levels very quickly. Fortunately, his senior position with his employer meant that he always had the benefit of business class, or even first-class travel, meaning that the in-flight service and the food provided to him, were always excellent.

Henry, one of his colleagues for whom Edwards had great respect, made his own observation: "I hope that there will be a decent bottle of wine involved as well!" he said. Edwards laughed; he knew that Henry had more to do with the European business of his construction group than he did. Born in Prague, as a small boy he had escaped from the Nazis on one of the trains organised by Sir Nicholas Winton, to take Jewish children to safety in England during the late 1930's.

Henry spoke at least five languages besides English, and had the kind of logical, calculating mind that Edwards always found very useful to connect with. Henry now worked, most of his time, in marketing behind the "Iron Curtain" that divided Europe. Some of his stories of his adventures, dealing with the Communist regimes there, were very well worth listening to.

"Drink wise, I am looking forward to a good Gin and Tonic, before the meal," responded Edwards.

Jones from Marketing, the third member of their party, made his contribution. "I hope that we get a good American steak," he said.

Jones was always enthusiastic; "I suppose you have to be, to work in Marketing," Edwards thought to himself.

After some ten minutes, they were collected by the Personal Assistant to the Director, who was to be their host. Dressed in a dark trouser suit, she seemed to be a typical New Yorker. Edwards had observed that they generally did not waste words, but, when they did speak, they usually said something that had some importance. She took them into the Executive Elevator which rapidly took them, non-stop, up to the top floor of the building. She showed them into the large dining room; it was luxuriously furnished and had original prints of old New York on its walls. The large table was set for six people, with fine place mats, silver cutlery, and finely cut glasses.

The windows gave a breath-taking view of Manhattan, which was added to by the fact that it was a bright, cloudless day. "He is running a little late," the Personal Assistant said. "He will be with you soon." She shut the door behind her.

"Looks good!" said Jones. "They have set the table for us very nicely."

The three colleagues took in the magnificent views from the large picture windows and spotted the Empire State Building, away in the distance. The door opened; it was a smartly dressed waitress carrying a silver tray. "Can I get you gentlemen something to drink?" she asked.

Edwards paused; he remembered that he was in the United States and that maybe they would not stock the pre-luncheon drinks that he was used to, back home in England. "What have you got please?" he asked.

"We have water, milk or orange juice," was the curt reply.

Edwards had nearly to stop himself from staggering backwards! The thought of the much-desired Gin and Tonic had vanished very quickly. There was consultation among the three men; "We will have three orange juices please," asked Edwards.

"At least, that way, we can imagine that there is something else in them," said Henry, grinning broadly.

"Well, I am sure that the food will be alright," said Jones, as always, the optimist.

3

They gathered around the windows again, with their orange juices, and admired the magnificent views. Suddenly, the door burst open and the Director, with two of his colleagues, entered. He looked a little harassed; it seemed perhaps that his previous meeting had not gone well. Unlike some Americans, he was not overweight.

He introduced himself, and then his two colleagues. The Director ordered himself a glass of water, and the two other Americans had glasses of milk. They were all dressed in very expensive suits, with fine button-down shirts and sober ties. But Edwards sensed a level of high, incipient stress about them.

Increasingly, they appeared to get more agitated. "Nothing that a stiff, alcoholic drink would not solve," thought Edwards. After talking about the reason for their visit for a few minutes, the British were quickly invited to sit down, and the Americans arranged themselves opposite them, on the other side of the table. "I suppose that these guys have to work very hard to justify their very high salaries," thought Edwards. "But they are really driving themselves into an early grave!"

The waitress reappeared to offer to each of them the choice of plain water or carbonated water with their food. Edwards decided to choose the carbonated water; at least it would give a little "sparkle" to the forthcoming meal! The Director operated a bell under the table, and three waiters immediately entered.

Each was carrying two plates, and each plate was covered by a silver cover, topped with a handle. One plate was placed on each place mat in front of each diner. The waiters then located themselves between each diner, so that each waiter could grasp two of the handles on the silver covers. The oldest of the waiters made a signal and together, in a co-ordinated movement, all the covers were lifted off the plates, simultaneously.

Beneath each cover, dwarfed by the large plates, was the smallest piece of Nouvelle Cuisine that Edwards had ever seen! The American Director took one look at what was on offer. "Gee! This is too much for me. Bring me some lettuce!" he demanded angrily.

The meal continued, but the conversation began to dry up; the banker's minds were obviously on other things. The main course was served: another nondescript piece of Nouvelle Cuisine, again of such a small size, that it was dwarfed by its plate. The desert course consisted of a bowl with the smallest smear of Chocolate Mousse inside it. By this time, Edwards had begun to suspect that there would be none of the normal coffee, liquors, and cigars that he was used to at the end of the meal. He was right!

As one man, the three Englishmen stood up, and thanked their American hosts for the meal. They were then escorted back down in the Executive Lift, to the ground floor, and out of the building. Out on the Wall Street sidewalk, Henry was the first to recover from the shock. He spoke first.

"Good God!" he said. "Let us go and find a good Bar, that serves food too, and get something decent to eat."

Jones nodded in agreement. "I think that they had other things on their minds, besides us. They seemed totally distracted," he said.

"Good idea, as always, Henry," agreed Edwards. "I think that we now have an afternoon free of meetings. After getting a proper lunch, we can get a cab to Central Park, and go for a walk there as it's a dry and sunny day. Then we can go to the Guggenheim Museum and see some pictures. I was there a few years ago, with my wife, but I would very much like to see it again." His colleagues eagerly agreed with his plan.

"I really felt sorry for those poor, rich bankers," said Henry perceptively, as they entered a nearby bar and restaurant. "They seemed to be totally stressed out!" he added.

The three colleagues ordered beers and then hamburgers. Edwards mentioned to them the quote from J. P. Morgan, Junior, that he had read; then he explained what he had found out from his research into the current salaries and bonuses now paid to this firm's senior bankers.

"I am not surprised to hear this now," said Henry. "Because of what they earn, they are so driven to make a success, that they probably work long hours in the office just to impress their bosses. They get very angry and stressed out about just being able to keep their jobs. They probably act dishonestly, and take short cuts as well, in order to get large bonuses. There must be so much rivalry among them that it is really like working in a jungle."

"Yes," said Jones. "They behave just like animals. It's eat or be eaten. Probably, they will soon turn to cannibalism!"

Edwards laughed. "I think that the current situation tends towards irresponsible behaviour and the breakdown of a decent work ethic," he said. "It leads naturally to individual greed, disorder, and financial breakdown. I can see what J. P. Morgan was getting at. Thank God the City of London is not like that," he added. "But I have a terrible feeling that it will, perhaps, not be long before it too becomes like Wall Street. If it does, it will be a great shame, and lead to all the same problems that, undoubtedly, this place has now developed."

Edwards did not know how right he was. Just over two years later, the City of London was shaken by what was then called "the Big Bang." The London Stock Exchange was de-regularised, and the long-existing City institutions had to rapidly change, or be bought up by foreign buyers. The two illustrious merchant banks that Edwards had worked for, and which had for years provided vital and excellent service to British and overseas companies, disappeared. One was bought by a major German bank, and the other by a very large American institution. The very capable stock broking firm that Edwards had also once worked for, was bought up by another major bank, which had its headquarters in Hong Kong.

By the mid-1990's, the same rampant capitalism that had developed in New York, had infected the City of London. Instead of friendly competition and honest and professional, objective expertise, what was on offer now was greed, intense competition, personal stress, and an all-consuming drive to make money. In time this brought a lack of a proper service, higher and higher fees and bonuses, increasing financial instability, fraud, and deceit!

The overpaid executives who now ran these organisations, had no loyalty to them, only to themselves, and their only interest was in increasing the enormous sums that they could earn. They did not understand the real need to provide a service to their clients, indeed they were not interested in doing so. Short-term profit, not professionalism, "was now King!"

4

The next morning, they flew to Washington. They were very lucky; they arrived there for the best week for the Cherry Blossom. Around the Capitol Building, the Washington Monument, and the Reflecting Pool, leading to the Lincoln Memorial, the cherry trees were in full flower. It was truly a beautiful sight! They took a walk up one side of the Reflecting Pool, and then down the other, rather like the Japanese do, to fully appreciate the beauty of this annual, but short-lived, flowering of the Cherry.

In the afternoon, they had a planned meeting at the International Finance Corporation. The IFC is a subsidiary of the World Bank and is the organisation which supports private sector development in many countries around the world. Increasingly, the British Government was beginning to try and privatise some of its major infrastructure projects. It was beginning to ask major construction companies, like the one that they worked for, to finance themselves in order to build what had previously been Government financed projects.

The construction companies were then allowed to own and operate these projects, either for a long period of time, or in perpetuity. Through this ownership, the companies were able, in time, to reimburse themselves, including the costs, interest, and profit, from the income that they could earn from the project that they had originally constructed. Other Governments were beginning to take the same approach, and the IFC was pleased to see them and offered their support and possible financial help for such privatised projects, in developing countries.

The following morning they had a meeting at the World Bank itself. After breakfast, Henry suggested that they should walk to their offices. It was another fine morning, and they agreed that, again, they would take a detour along the Reflecting Pool to the Lincoln Memorial and then back again, along the other side.

"I have heard about the flowering of these cherry trees," said Edwards. "But I have missed them, every time that I have been here before."

"It is really a magnificent sight," said Henry. "Only in Japan, I think, can you get the same experience." Edwards agreed with him.

They entered the World Bank building; a schedule of meetings had already been set up for them by the London office of the bank. This international institution is owned jointly by its participating member Governments. The World Bank has many departments; some of them dealt with certain types of projects, and some dealt with different regions of the world. So the men from London had a series of meetings, covering both project types, and various regions of the world, starting in the morning and continuing into late in the afternoon. The World Bank's London office had added a final meeting with the Administration Department. "So that you can give them an overview," had been the comment from the lady in London who had set up all these meetings for Edwards.

They had a very busy morning, and then took a quick lunch at a nearby Deli. The rest of the afternoon went by quickly; Edwards was making careful notes of each meeting. They were due to fly back to London the following morning, and he knew that he would be asked to prepare a full report on their visit, for the Group's Directors, immediately upon his return.

Their last meeting, with the Administration Department, was a strange one. The World Bank had to try and employ as many different nationalities as possible, from all its member countries. Their previous meetings had been with a great mix of different people, from a great variety of nationalities. But now, they were confronted by three tough-looking American men, and they seemed more concerned with who they had seen in their organisation, what they thought of them, and what had been said. They were not interested at all in what their group of companies could offer. They did, however, ask some very searching questions about some of the projects that their group were already doing, in certain countries.

At last, this last meeting, which had gone on for over ninety minutes, was over. They left the World Bank building, and Edwards turned to his two colleagues.

"That last meeting went on for a bit," he said. "They were certainly asking us some really tough questions."

Jones agreed. "It was totally different from the other meetings we had," he said. "They just sat and questioned us. These guys gave us the Third Degree!"

Henry's eyes twinkled; "Didn't you realise who they were?" he asked.

"No," answered Edwards. "But they seemed to be very knowledgeable about us and our group already."

Henry smiled. "C.I.A., the Central Intelligence Agency," he said knowingly. "They have an office in the World Bank, as the Americans insist on it. They always want to know who outside visitors, like us, are meeting, and what has been discussed. They gather in as much intelligence that they can, from everyone that they can meet." Their walk back to their hotel, past the flowering cherry trees, was relaxing. They were all looking forward to a good dinner after an intensive day of work, with a "decent bottle of wine," as Henry would say!

Over dinner, they discussed the meetings they had taken part in earlier that day. "It is strange," said Edwards "to compare the people we saw in New York, with the people we saw today. So many of the people we saw today, irrespective of their nationality, seemed genuinely concerned with trying to help the world and how we could help them to do so. They were all real, international public servants."

"Whereas, in Wall Street, they were only concerned about themselves, and making money," interjected Henry. "It's called Capitalism by the way, and the more I see of it actually working, the more I really have to wonder if Karl Marx was not right after all? Not that I could have said that earlier, to our friends from the C.I.A.!" he quickly added, grinning broadly.

THE BATTLE

By Thomas Marshall, RN
With a Foreword by Christopher Spencer

"The past is not dead. In fact it is not even past."
– William Faulkner.

Thomas Marshall joined the Royal Navy at the end of the 19th century. At the beginning of the last century, Tom was serving in the Far East Squadron and visited Hong Kong, China, Singapore, Japan, Burma (Myanmar,) and Ceylon, (Sri Lanka,) many times. In his time with the Royal Navy, he also visited Canadian and Russian ports. In 1903 he joined the crew of the newly built and commissioned armoured cruiser H.M.S. Monmouth, and soon returned to the Far East.

Fortunately for him, just before the outbreak of the First World War, he was transferred to H.M.S. Cornwall, another of the ten "Monmouth Class" armoured cruisers built for the Royal Navy in the first decade of the 20th century. He continued to serve on the Cornwall for the rest of the First World War, where he rose to the rank of Master of Arms. He retired from the Royal Navy in the early 1920's. At some stage, in the later 1920's, he became my maternal grandmother's lover and, some years later, she left her husband to live with him.

When I stayed with my grandmother as a boy, part of that experience that I well remember, were the marvellous stories Tom used to tell me of the happenings on board ship, and about his many visits to far distant lands.

The Battle of Coronel on 1st November 1914, off the coast of Central Chile, was the first major naval engagement of the War. It was a German victory under Vice-Admiral Maximilian Reichsgraf von Spee, who commanded the German East Asia Squadron. H.M.S Monmouth, (on which Tom had served for many years) and H.M.S Good Hope were both lost, with all hands. Over 1,500 British sailors died, including their commander Rear-Admiral Sir Christopher Cradock. The German Squadron then entered the Atlantic and the British sent a large force to track down and destroy the Germans, which included H.M.S. Cornwall.

The First Battle of the Falkland Islands was fought off Port Stanley on 8th December 1914 between the British and German cruiser fleets. The British were commanded by Vice-Admiral Doveton Sturdee, and the engagement started when the Germans attempted to raid, and then destroy, the major British coaling

THE BATTLE

and provisions base at Port Stanley. This sea battle proved a sweet revenge for the Royal Navy; four of the German naval vessels were sunk with only a few survivors. Vice-Admiral Graf von Spee and his two sons, who were serving on different ships, were all killed, along with over 1,800 other German sailors. The fifth German cruiser, the Dresden, was found shortly after the battle by H.M.S. Glasgow and Kent, and its crew were forced to scuttle their ship. The German East Asia Squadron had been completely destroyed.

The true story below is taken from a typewritten letter, in my possession, dated 9th December 1914, the day after the First Battle of the Falkland Islands. It is from Thomas Marshall on H.M.S Cornwall, and is addressed to his father in Shropshire.

> H.M.S. Cornwall,
> Falkland Islands.
> 9th December 1914.

Dear Dad,

I think I told you the other day that, if Graf von Spee came this way, he would probably get the surprise of his life and I was not far out. Our fleet consisting of the Battle Cruisers Invincible and Inflexible, and the Cruisers Cornwall, Kent, Bristol, Glasgow, and Carnarvon, only arrived here on Monday. We were preparing to coal and fill up with provisions etc., when on Tuesday morning, the 8$^{th\,of}$ December, Graf von Spee with the Cruisers Scharnhorst, Gneisenau, Leipzig, Nürnberg, and Dresden arrived here looking for trouble. As I daresay you have read in the papers, he got all he asked for.

He arrived about 8 a.m. and sent a couple of Cruisers close in to the shore to have a look round, with the intention of bringing in the whole fleet that night to bombard the place. As soon as he was spotted by the lookouts on the hill, we started to get up steam. They soon spotted our smoke and started to get a move on to get away. By the time we got out of harbour, they were about 20 miles away going hell for leather to the Southward. We got after them on time, the Battle Cruisers, of course, being the fastest, soon drew ahead, but they did not get very far ahead of us.

We cleared the harbour about 10.30 a.m. and by noon the Battle Cruisers were going about 28 knots and the remainder about 24 knots per hour. The poor old Carnarvon was the only lame duck; they could only get about 20 knots out of her and we soon left them behind hull down, (she managed to get in at the finish though.) The Bristol was despatched to chase the enemy's colliers, so that left six of us to chase the Germans. By this time they were going all out and we were after them.

About 1 p.m. our Battle Cruisers opened fire with their 12 inch guns at extreme long range and soon after the enemy's two big ships opened fire in return. We were watching them through our glasses, but it came on a trifle hazy about then. After a short time our ships got their range and I think both the Scharnhorst, (Flagship,) and the Gneisenau, got a decent clout each. Anyway, they turned off at right angles and made a run for it. About half an hour previous to this, the Leipzig, Nürnburg, and Dresden turned off to the right and we, the Cornwall, Kent, and Glasgow, turned in pursuit of them. By the time their big ships turned to run, they, (the big ones,) were a long way from us, about 20 miles or so. We could only see their smoke going parallel to us, so could not see what they were doing. We were going as hard as we could to tear after the others and very gradually overhauling them. Of course, they were very fast and running for their lives, so wanted some catching. However, our fellows below worked like slaves and fairly lifted her along.

The Glasgow, a new Light Cruiser, is very fast and she gradually drew ahead of us. At about 3 p.m. she got the range of, and opened fire on, the Leipzig, who immediately replied. They exchanged a few broadsides without doing much damage, as far as we could see. However the Leipzig soon got the Glasgow's distance and the latter hauled off and ceased firing. Soon after 4 p.m. we got in range of the Leipzig and set about her. She fought a splendid running action, but we were too good for her. We hit a funnel out of her, after a time, and that reduced her speed. Sometime after the action commenced, we started to pelt her with high explosive shells and set her on fire in several places. Only the misty weather saved her as long as she did last.

About 8 o'clock she ceased firing and by that time, she was burning like a Living Hell. One of her masts was gone, blown clean out of her, two of her funnels and half of the third knocked away. The marvel of it was how she floated at all, or, how floating, anyone could live in her. We gradually closed in on her, when we were pretty sure she was too bad to wing us with a torpedo. At about 9 o'clock we sent out some boats to see if we could save any of the survivors.

The Glasgow also closed in and sent some boats; they could not go right alongside for fear of her sinking or blowing up.

Out of 276 men who went into action, only 16 remained and they jumped over the side and were picked up by the boats. About 9.20 she quietly heeled over and went down without any fuss. Some of the survivors could speak English and they said there was hardly a square yard in her that was not ripped with our shell. How they escaped is a mystery to them. Above the waterline, she was just a mass of twisted, tortured metal.

THE BATTLE

At about 6.30 p.m. we got news that that the Sharnhorst and Gneisnau had been sunk by our two big Cruisers, and the Kent had just arrived and reported she has sunk the Nurnberg. The Dresden is very fast and, having a good start, managed to escape this time, but I guess it won't be long before she comes under the hammer. However 4 out of 5, and 2 colliers, is not a bad bag for one day and the Good Hope and Monmouth, which were sunk by them on November 1st are avenged. No survivors were saved from the Scharnhorst; 100 were saved from the Gneisenau; 16 from Leipzig, and 7 from Nürnberg. So, there must have been about 2,000 of them wiped out altogether.

From what those fellows that we saved said, Von Spee was going to sweep the ocean clear of us; since he sunk the Good Hope and Monmouth his head had swelled considerably. It was the biggest surprise he had ever had when our two Battle Cruisers appeared. He was under the impression that he had a soft thing on, wherein he erred somewhat. I guess by this time, their great War Lord is feeling somewhat sick about it.

The marvellous part is that our fleet had so few casualties; the Invincible had one killed, Inflexible nil, Kent 5, Cornwall nil, Glasgow 1. Some of the ships had a few severely wounded, but we, by a miracle, escaped without a single man having a scratch. They punched our old tub about some, we have a few holes and a good many dents. They played a merry tattoo on our sides occasionally, when they got the range. But most of their shells landed on our armour and exploded harmlessly. Our Captain fought the ship in great style. They never kept our range long through dodging about so much, whereas we kept theirs all right. They put up a good scrap and fought whilst they had a gun to fight with and, so I hear, did the remainder. But we were too heavy for them and simply wiped them up.

We have heard that our big ships were punching holes in theirs big enough to drive a motor car through. The surprise was so beautifully arranged that it must have taken their breath away! They had not the faintest idea that we had two big Cruisers down here. As I said, they thought they had a soft thing on. One of the survivors from the Gneisenau says that when a Signalman reported to the Captain that two tripod mast ships were coming out, the Captain called him a liar! They were the nearest ship to ours and, when they were sure of it, they made a signal to Admiral Von Spee in the Scharnhorst telling him. He made a reply: "Impossible." However, he knew all about it a little later on.

Am still going on A.1. It is pretty cold down here. Coming down from the Tropics, we feel it a good deal. But it is fine and healthy. We may be chasing around for some little time, so don't be surprised if you don't hear from me for a week or two. Our mails down here are irregular at the best of times and Von Spee had disorganised things more.

Your Loving Son, Tom.

ANOTHER COUNTRY

"The past is a foreign country; they do things differently there." Opening sentence of The Go-Between by J. P. Hartley.

1

It was a sparkling, sunny morning in November in the year 1934. It was warm enough outside for the young couple to have a small table and two chairs made up on their narrow hotel balcony, to have breakfast. Just a simple one; croissants, country butter, and homemade jams, washed down with the excellent French coffee. Compared with what they knew in England, the daylight was incredibly bright. The young bride had first to shade her eyes, and then went back inside to fetch her fashionable sunglasses, which had been purchased at great expense before she had left home. "It was true, the sea really was azure here," she thought, as her eyes took in the beautiful, broad sweep of the Baie des Anges.

Their journey had started in rural Shropshire. In the morning they had been married at their local church, then a Wedding Reception had been held at the Forest Glen Pavilion, located at the base of the Wrekin. Her father, as always, had been a little mean, although he had no need to be so. She had been brought up in a large house, well-furnished, and with a number of live-in staff. She was only now learning to dress and undress by herself; until her marriage, she had always had her own lady's maid to help her carry out these daily tasks.

Her father was conscious of his high social status and had packed the Reception with his friends. Many of them were local notables, and the Mayor of the Borough was, of course, also in attendance. The guests included many of his brother Freemasons and their wives. His was an ancient Huguenot family who had fled to this part of England, from France, after the Saint Bartholomew's Day Massacre in 1572. His hobby was to collect the locally produced Coalport China, and several of the reception rooms of his house had great cabinets full of his large collection of this fine, beautifully decorated, local product. Some twenty years later he was himself to become the Mayor of this ancient Borough of Wenlock, and then to be appointed a Freeman. The Borough could trace its history back to the eighth century when lands were collected by the Priory of Wenlock; these lands were then confirmed by the Doomsday Book, and by a Royal Charter given by King Richard the Lionheart in 1198. In 1468 King Edward the Fourth granted the Charter that first mentioned the Borough of Wenlock which, at its height, was the second largest borough in England outside of London.

Her mother was from a moneyed Welsh family who had settled in this part of Shropshire. When her parents had died young, she and her younger sister had been brought up by two maiden aunts who lived in Dulwich, in South London. They had received a private education at the hands of tutors, and when they were old enough and had received their parent's inheritance, which had previously been held in trust, they had returned to Shropshire. She had married this prominent local man, and her sister had married the owner of the very profitable local brewery.

The number of the Groom's guests had been small; his Best Man of course, some of his friends, some colleagues from the local bank where he worked, and just a few of his brothers and sisters. Unfortunately, both of his parents were already dead, but, as a family they were well established with large land holdings in the west of the county. Altogether his mother had given birth to twelve children, one daughter had died in infancy, and one of his older brothers had been killed in the First World War. All his sisters had married other wealthy farmers and each of his brothers had inherited sufficient land from their parents, to set up their own farms.

His new wife knew that instead of land to farm, he had inherited money from his parents. As the youngest brother, he had been selected by his parents for a different kind of life. Sent away to a boarding school at the age of six, he had almost pined away there, from missing a life with his family back home. In the hard, Shropshire winters, the young boy's dormitories had been freezing. They had to break the ice on top of the bowls of water in which they had to wash every morning. From his preparatory school, he was sent on to a Public School in the north-west of the county; it was really not all that far from his home, but he was only allowed to visit his family during the school holidays.

Founded in 1884, his Public School had an emphasis on sport. He had once broken his foot while playing rugby for one of the school teams. The medical attention had been rudimentary; the foot had never been properly set and, for the rest of his life, he had walked with a limp. During the forthcoming Second World War, he had been turned down by all three Armed Forces because of it.

Instead, he had had to stay as a civilian and do the work of three men because so many other men had been sent away to fight. But he had excelled academically, indeed, in his Sixth Form, he had won a National Prize in an Essay Competition where pupils from all the Public Schools in England had submitted their work. When it came to finding him a job, it had been simple: his father was a very good customer of the local bank, and he just had a word with his bank manager. The next month, his youngest son was found a job in another branch of that bank, not all that far away from his home.

As soon as he was old enough, he had purchased a motorcycle and first rode it from school, when he was allowed out, along the country roads to his home for a rare weekend with his family. When he was eighteen, he had purchased a sports car; he now looked dashing, with his fair hair, blue eyes, and his growing moustache. He enjoyed playing golf and playing cards with his friends. He Rode to Hounds and enjoyed shooting and, above all, fishing. He attended the nearest Horse Races and the local Point-to-Points.

For the local country girls, he was considered a "good catch." He was public- school educated, handsome, obviously well-off, and sporty. What more could a girl desire in a husband? After a few years, he was moved to another branch of the same bank. This branch was set alongside the Gorge, which the great River Severn had carved out. Thrown across the gorge was a historic iron bridge. It was the first such bridge that had been made of iron in the world and had been completed in 1781. His social life grew and there were always parties, dances, and visits to friends, with several girls becoming interested in his attentions.

2

But he had now made his own choice of his bride; he had bought her an expensive diamond engagement ring, from a leading London jeweller, and they had now been engaged for an acceptable twelve months period before their marriage. He was content that he was marrying a girl from a respectable, well-off and socially well-placed family from this part of the county. He was in love with his chosen future wife and he thought that she seemed to adore him. As far as her parents were concerned, he was a little in awe of his future father-in-law, but liked his future wife's mother who seemed, very much, to welcome him into their family and had expressed the wish that they should be married as soon as they wanted.

After the Reception, their hired driver and car had taken them to a small hotel in the nearby town, where the new husband had booked a room for them to change in. They were still bashful, and she occupied the room first to change, while he waited downstairs. Then he used the room to change into his new, smart, three-piece suit. The car took them the short ride to the local station, and then they took a branch line train to the main line junction. Even on the branch line they travelled in a reserved first-class compartment to themselves. Then they had caught the express train to London.

ANOTHER COUNTRY

Looking out of the window of their first-class reserved compartment, she had watched the English countryside speed by. She loved her new husband, but she was both excited and anxious about what must happen next. She had really lived a sheltered life. She knew nothing about the physical side of marriage; her mother had told her nothing about it. She had merely complained about her father, and "what a beast" he was. Her mother had always asked to sleep with her, except when her father had entered their bedroom and took her away, in order to assert his conjugal rights.

But she knew that her mother had a different view of another man. She had been forced by her mother to visit him with her, many times, to give the appearance of an innocent social visit. Nevertheless, her mother had encouraged her only child to marry at the earlies opportunity. Her father had made it clear that practically any man, was not good enough to marry his daughter, including her new husband. This was despite the fact that he was charming, well-educated, had family money, and a well-paid position in the local branch of a major bank. But, she had just turned the age of twenty-one, and she no longer required her father's approval to marry. So he had to grudgingly accept that she would now marry the man that she had chosen.

Arriving at the terminus, they glimpsed the great Arch outside Euston Station as their taxi took them to their hotel. He had been to London many times before, but she had not. Although it was a little out of their way, he asked the taxi driver to sweep around Trafalgar Square and then down The Mall, to pass Buckingham Palace. The taxi soon arrived at their first-class hotel, set on the north bank of the Thames. It was where he always stayed when he came up to London. She hung back modestly as he registered them at the Reception Desk, and then their ample luggage was carried up for them to their room. The room was luxurious; it partly overlooked the river, and she noted the presence of the waiting, large, double bed.

The next morning, they took their time over their excellent English breakfast. She smiled at her new husband, for that was now what he really was. It had not been as bad as she had expected; just a short, sharp pain followed by an increasing pleasure. After breakfast, they took a taxi for some leisurely sight-seeing, and then visits to some West End stores to buy a few essentials for their Honeymoon that they had not been able to buy at home. That evening they had dinner at the Café Royal, in Regent Street.

The next morning they rose early, breakfasted in their room, and then took another taxi with their luggage, to Victoria Station.

ANOTHER COUNTRY

They caught the early Boat Train. It was to be a long day; the train to Dover, the short Channel crossing to Calais, and then the train to the Gare du Nord in Paris. From there, they took a taxi to the Gare de Lyon. With the help of Thomas Cook, who had supplied the tickets and the detailed itinerary, he had planned their journey meticulously. They would arrive at Le Buffet de la Gare de Lyon just in time for a late, light lunch. He wanted his new bride to experience the finest of French cuisine, in the finest of French settings.

Le Buffet had been created for the Exposition Universelle in 1900. Each ornate dining room was themed to represent cities and regions in France, and was decorated by forty-one murals, painted by some of the most popular artists of the time. The large room was, overall, the most beautiful example of La Belle Epoque. He had deliberately asked for a small table, close to the mural which showed their final destination, so that she could see it as they ate.

They had plenty of time to catch their next train, from the same station. Rather than taking this train at Calais, he had booked them a sleeping compartment to start from Paris. They dressed for dinner, and joined their fellow passengers in the ornate Dining Car, where a five course dinner, complemented with fine wines, was served. The dishes were each served on fine, blue china, with silver cutlery and, after the food, coffee, cigars and liquors were, of course, available. The Sleeping Cars were painted blue, with gold trim, and were operated by the Compagnie Internationale des Wagons-Lits. Each Car had only ten sleeping compartments, with one attendant assigned to each Sleeping Car.

The height of the season for Le Train Bleu, as it was known, was between November and April when many travellers escaped the British winter to spend their time on the French Riviera. Overnight, the train made stops at Dijon, Châlons, and Lyon, before reaching Marseilles early the next morning. As the passengers returned to the Dining Car for their breakfasts, the train followed the spectacular line along the coast of the Cote d'Azur. Saint-Raphael, Juan-les-Pines, Antibes, and Cannes came and went. The young couple alighted at Nice, letting the train continue on to Monte-Carlo, and then to its final stop of Menton, close to the Italian border.

Nice railway station was completed in 1867; it was built in a Louis XIII style, richly decorated, with stone sculptures and a forged steel domed roof. It was a grand destination in itself, and there was an ornate Buffet, encircling balconies, a big clock, and great, cut-glass chandeliers. From the station, the Bridegroom hailed a taxi to the Hotel Beau Rivage. Built in 1860, over the years, this hotel had had many famous guests, including Henri Matisse, Anton Chekhov, Frederick Nietzsche, and F. Scott Fitzgerald. Set on the Promenade des Anglais, it had its own private beach, complete with an outside restaurant and bar.

The couple were shown to their large, luxurious room overlooking the Baie des Anges, with its small balcony jutting out from the front of the hotel. Their many cases were brought up to their room, but they did not begin to unpack immediately. Instead, they each had a bath in their en-suite bathroom to freshen up from their long journey. Only then did they begin to think about unpacking. But, the Bride was anxious to walk out onto the Promenade, in the warm, November sunshine.

The Bridegroom laughed at her indulgently, "Alright then," he said. "We have plenty of time, over a month here. In any case, we can ask for the Room Maid to unpack our suitcases."

3

Their next seven days were restful and blissful. That first day they had easily found their way across the broad road and on to the Promenade des Anglais, for a short walk. Then they went down the steps to the hotel's private beach. It was warm, at least sixty-five degrees Fahrenheit, dry, and sunny. They sat on two loungers, drawn together beside the sea at the hotel's outside bar, and enjoyed a bottle of the finest, chilled Champagne, with a light lunch.

The people of Nice are surprisingly fond of the English, but they have every reason to be so. Starting in the eighteenth century, the English aristocracy took to spending their winters in Nice, and established it as a premier seaside resort. There was soon a permanent English community living there. In 1820, a particularly harsh winter brought an influx of beggars from other parts of France and then, with the failure of the harvest, deprivation too for the local population.

The English community proposed a useful project to employ them: the construction of a walkway alongside the sea. It was paid for by the English community, and organised by the Reverend Lewis Way and the members of the Holy Trinity Anglican Church in Nice. The walkway was first called "The English Way" but, after the annexation of Nice from Italy by France in 1860, it was renamed La Promenade des Anglais.

On their second full day, the young couple turned right and walked slowly along the Promenade to the Hotel Negresco, for lunch. This hotel, with its prominent pink dome, had been constructed in 1912. It was named after its Romanian owner

Henri Negresco who died bankrupt after the First World War, as a direct result of his hotel being commandeered for use as a hospital during that war. But it was now, probably, the most famous hotel in Nice. It was designed by the great architect of La Belle Epoque, Édouard-Jean Niermans, and built to attract only the most wealthy of clients. The spectacular, huge crystal chandelier in its Royal Lounge, had been commissioned by Tsar Nicholas II, who was then unable to take its delivery due to the Russian October Revolution of 1917.

The next day, they turned left along the Promenade and walked to La Palais de la Jetee. This amazing construction had been commissioned by the Council of Nice in the 1870's; it was inspired by the Crystal Palace in London and was specifically intended to replicate the Victorian piers that were then being constructed in various British seaside resorts. But, it was to be bigger and better, and especially targeted towards gaining more British visitors. Unfortunately, the building was delayed, and it was not finally completed until 1891. Built, again in the flamboyant Belle Epoque style, it boasted a band stand, a concert hall, a theatre, walkways, restaurants, shops, and lounges which all served English afternoon tea. It was to be demolished by the Germans during the Second World War, in an act of philistine vengeance.

Again the young couple took a light lunch, and then booked to attend an operetta at the La Palais theatre that evening. Every night, they could see the great illuminated dome of La Palais from their hotel balcony, and the sound of music and laughter drifted from it, across the bay, and through their open balcony window.

There was no shortage of things to do; they soon found out the delights of the Old Town with its narrow alleyways, small squares, shops, and restaurants. There, souvenirs of many types could be bought and a cheaper lunch, with a bottle of good, local wine, could be purchased. On six days of the week, there was a crowded flower and vegetable market here, and even at this time of year, the colour and scents of the flowers brought in from the surrounding hills produced a virtual "Heaven on Earth!"

Then, there were some churches to visit; Nice's Roman Catholic Cathedral and, of course, the great, Russian Orthodox Saint Nicholas Cathedral. This was the largest, Eastern Orthodox cathedral in Western Europe, opened in 1912 thanks to the generosity of Tsar Nicholas II. The Russian community had always been strong in Nice and now, nearly twenty years after the Revolution, many émigré Russian aristocrats had established themselves in France, with apartments in Paris, and seaside villas on the Cote d'Azur.

One day, at the insistence of the husband, the couple took a local train to explore Monte-Carlo, and to visit its famous Casino, built in the Beaux Arts style in the previous century, along with its adjoining opera house. Then, they took a taxi up the hill to visit the Palace of Monaco's ruling Grimaldi family, and the nearby Monte-Carlo Cathedral.

4

It was at breakfast, on their eight day, that it happened. The Head Waiter approached their usual table, carrying a silver tray. He bowed, "Bonjour, Madame," he said, and then in his polished English, "There is a letter for you." She took the letter off the silver tray; it bore a British stamp and it was surprisingly thin. She recognised, at once, that the address was in her Mother's handwriting. She opened it carefully, and took out the single sheet of notepaper inside. She read it curiously, then let out a strangled cry. Tears welded up in her eyes, and she held her head in her other hand.

"Whatever is the matter?" her husband cried out. Several of their fellow guests looked at them in concern. In answer, she handed him the single sheet of paper. It bore no address, but was dated the day that they had left London for Paris. It was very short and straight to the point.

"Dear Joan," he read. "I am writing to you to let you know that I have left your Father. I cannot live with that Beast any more. Now that you have left, I can, at last, leave this house. I have left him and run away with Tom. Do not try and find me. You will never find me. With My Love, Mother."

They abandoned their breakfast, and he supported his sobbing wife back up to their room. She lay down on their bed, and he tried to comfort her as best as he could. At last, she cried herself to sleep. He moved to a chair overlooking the sea. He had hurriedly thrust the letter, in its envelope, into a pocket of his jacket. He now took it out and checked the envelope. Yes, it was addressed to his wife. His mind was in a turmoil but he tried to think logically. He looked at the postmark, could this give a clue as to where his Mother-in-Law had gone? But, the letter had been posted in the town in which his wife had grown up. His Mother-in-Law could have posted it there before she left that town, for the very last time.

He took the single sheet of paper out of the envelope and read it again, and then again. He could not believe what he was reading. He had married into one of the leading families in that part of the county, where he now lived and worked. There had been absolutely no sign that there had been unhappiness or instability in the marriage of his wife's parents. The status of his new Father-in-Law had been undoubted. He really did not know what to say to his new wife, or what to do.

She slept on. At lunchtime he ordered some sandwiches, coffee and some wine to be brought to their room. He tried to interest her in having something to eat or drink. He had a sudden idea; "Would you like some Cognac?" he asked. She shook her head. He poured her some coffee and passed her a sandwich. She just nibbled at it, but drank the coffee gratefully.

"Do you mind if I ask you some questions?" he asked quietly, trying to be as tactful as he could. Her eyes, red with crying, looked at him for the first time. She knew that this would be an important moment in their short marriage.

"Alright," she replied quietly.

"You did not tell me that anything was wrong between your parents," he began. Then he realised that it sounded that he was blaming her, which he did not want to do. "Did you know about their problems?" he ended up asking, rather lamely.

She looked at him again, but this time her gaze did not falter. She knew that she had to be very honest with him now, if only to save her own marriage. "Yes, I knew," she said quietly. "It has been going on for years, but I never believed that it would come to this. I did not want to tell you because, really, it was their personal business. Also, I admit, that I was frightened that it would put you off me."

She began to sob again, and he sat down on the bed, and put his arm around her. "I understand," he said quietly. "I am not blaming you. It has just come as such a shock to me too."

"I am so sorry that you have been brought into this," she managed to get out between her sobs. "If I had known that this is what she was going to do, as soon as we were married, I would never have married you."

He held her close, with both his arms, to comfort her. But there was one more question that he had. "Who is this man, Tom?" he asked quietly.

Her sobbing broke out again. "He was a friend of hers," she answered. "When I was younger, we both used to go and see him at the same time, every week. He lives locally, with his widowed mother. He does not work, but lives off his Navy pension. He served in the Royal Navy for many years. He is a most interesting man, who has travelled the world. He also took part in some of the sea battles of the last war."

"Did you suspect that there was anything between them?" he asked, as gently as he could.

"Yes," came the sobbing reply. "Usually, when we went to see him, his mother was out. My mother asked me to sit in the window, and keep looking down the hill, to see if I could see my father coming up it, towards Tom's house. I was to warn her, if I saw him, while she went upstairs with Tom!"

"I am so very sorry," was all that he could respond to her last answer.

5

That evening they had dinner in their room; she said that she could not face the Dining Room with, no doubt, the other hotel guests looking at her curiously, or even enquiring how she was. On one of his short visits downstairs, the husband had already been approached by the Hotel Manager. "Is Madame well, Monsieur?" had been his polite enquiry. "May I call a doctor for her?"

He knew that he had to say something and that whatever he said, would slowly filter around the hotel. "No, thank you," he replied. "She has just received some bad news from home."

All perfectly true, but then he lied. "It was her favourite Aunt. Unfortunately, she has just passed away." Then he made a firm decision. "But we will stay here, as planned," he said. "We will not be returning back to England early, for the funeral."

The next morning, as well, she still did not want to face the Dining Room. They ordered breakfast in their room. He knew that he had to get her out; it was fortunately again a bright and warm day outside. But first, he opened the double doors to their balcony and put a chair ready, out there for her, so that she could enjoy the fresh sea air. "Sit there for a while, but then I think that a little walk in the sunshine, will do you good," he told her. By mid-morning, he had persuaded her to take a walk along the Promenade, and it seemed natural that she took his arm to support herself.

They talked quietly. "What are we to do?" she asked him.

"I have decided," he replied firmly, "that we shall stay here. Nothing will be served by going back to England early. You need both rest and the change of scene to recuperate. It has been a great shock to both you, and to me."

"But what about my Father?" she asked.

"You must write to him and tell him that you have heard from your Mother, but that she did not tell you where she has gone." She seemed to hesitate. "If we go back now, it could be unpleasant, and he might, just, partly blame you for your Mother leaving," he added. "He is a prominent man and he has many friends who will help him. I am sure that he will be able to cope with what has happened, by himself."

They walked back to the hotel's seaside bar. "Let us have some light lunch," he said, "and some wine. It will help you. The sound of the sea will help you as well. It is always very soothing for the nerves." They sat in silence, eating their lunch, and enjoying the wine, in the warm sunshine.

At last, she turned to him. "You are right," she said. "We will stay here and try and enjoy the rest of our Honeymoon. But, I am so sorry that this has happened. I feel that you will never be able to forgive me, for not telling you the truth. I feel that, somehow, I have misled you."

"My Darling," he replied to her, taking her hand. "How could I ever blame you? It is not your fault, in any way. If anything, it is your Mother who is to blame. She has been so selfish to do this, so soon after we were married, and without letting you know what she was going to do."

They stayed for three more weeks on the Cote d'Azur; the weather was just splendid. Gradually, the great cloud, caused by what had happened, began to lift. They visited, again, the places where they had already been; perhaps it was an attempt to regain the happiness and the certainty that they had felt before the letter had arrived. As well as enjoying the delights of Nice, for a change, they took a local train to the west and visited Cannes and Antibes.

Fortunately, he was due to restart his work with the bank at a different branch, this time in the city of Worcester. Their planned return to England would be to that city, and it would be a new start for both of them. First, they would have to stay in a hotel, paid for by his bank, until they found a house to buy or rent. All their belongings could then be sent on to this new abode; their first real home, as a married couple.

The past can never truly be forgotten. But, where it is unpleasant, it can hopefully, over time, be carefully eased from the immediate memory. This can be done perhaps, by later happier memories and, of course, with love.

SEA DREAMS

"Now seaward-bound for health they gain'd a coast.
All sand and cliff and deep in-running cave."
— Alfred Lord Tennyson.

1

The boy's eyes took in the broad vista of the view. He was sitting on a rock in a rather overgrown section of his grandmother's large, back garden. The house itself was built on an isolated hill, and he was at its highest point. In front of him, in the distance, loomed the massive bulk of Holyhead Mountain. Closer, there was a view of the Inland Sea, between the main island of Anglesey and Holy Island, on which this mountain stood. On either side, was a view of the flat, ancient peneplain of the main island. Behind, in the distance, could be seen the majestic mountains of Snowdonia.

Except for the crying of the seabirds, there was silence. Satisfied that the magnificent views were still there, the boy cuddled the tufted hair on the chest of the Welsh Sheep Dog that belonged to his grandmother, and which had accompanied him on his solitary walk around the back garden. He sat there for a few more minutes to enjoy his solitude, before returning, by the steep pathway, to the house.

He was on his summer holidays from school, and he always spent them at his grandmother's house. His mother had brought him, on the express train from their home, but had then returned, leaving her son in the care of her mother. Britain was still trying to recover from the ravages of the Second World War; life seemed monotonous with little joy within it, and food rationing was still in place. But here, this grey and depressed world seemed to have little hold over events, and one could happily live within pure nature.

Even the train journey from their home in a small Shropshire town, was always exciting. First the short train journey, on a small branch line, to the main line station. Then they boarded the express train, bound for Holyhead, and the boats that one could then take on to Ireland. The great steam locomotive thundered into the station, pulling its numerous carriages. Smoke and steam bellowed up. The burning smell of soot filled the air. Eagerly, they had found seats in a carriage; the train was already nearly full because it arrived at the port at a popular time, to catch one of the boats for the overnight crossing of the Irish Sea.

SEA DREAMS

The boy loved to look out of the window of the speeding train. Soon the rolling English countryside would give way to the railway line, high above the sea, along the North Wales coast. Then they passed beneath the great, medieval walls of Conwy Castle. A series of tunnels, cut through the cliffs high above the sea, brought them to the small university city of Bangor. But the most exciting part of the journey, for the boy, was still to come. Ahead lay the great Britannia Tubular Railway Bridge, designed in wrought iron by Robert Stephenson, and opened in 1850. It crossed the Menai Strait, to the island of Anglesey.

On either side of the bridge stood two giant stone loins, which he always looked out for. He knew then that the journey was nearly over. It was just a simple run across the flat fields of the island, before they were deposited at the small station in the nearest village. It was still nearly three miles to his grandmother's house. The local taxi man, who they knew well, took them to it with their cases, in his ancient car, along the narrow lanes.

At last, they arrived at the isolated bungalow, set high on a giant rock, with its magnificent views. There they would receive a warm welcome. His grandmother, despite her years, remained active and sprightly. The man, whom she had never married, but whose name she had taken by Deed Poll, was also there to welcome them. Indeed, she could never marry him, as she still remained married to the father of the boy's mother. She had left her husband in 1934, and had disappeared to live, in this wild place, with her lover.

The house had to be self-sufficient; rainwater was gathered in large tanks around the house. Rather than letting this water be used up, every day the boy helped to carry large metal jugs to the well, situated in the middle of a field, some distance away. They had the farmer's permission to use this water source, and the old pump always gave plenty of exercise to the boy, as he used it to force the pure water up from its natural reservoir, deep below. Then there was the difficult task of carrying the now heavy jugs, filled with water, back to the house.

This water was used for all their cooking and washing needs. A bath would be taken in a tin bath, and the water would be heated in a large kettle on the kitchen range, above a coal fire. In the winter, a bath could be taken in front of the coal fire in the main room. Their natural needs were met by a chemical toilet in one of the outbuildings, which had to be regularly emptied by the man, into a deep hole that he had dug for this purpose, in part of the back garden.

In the winter, the only heating for the house were open fires. Coal could be burnt only, that was, if they could get the coalman to deliver it all the way to this isolated house. Or logs could be supplied by some of the local farms. At night, the house was lit by paraffin lamps or candles. The indoor entertainment was limited to reading, playing games, or listening to the large, old wireless, contained in its brown case, and powered by a heavy accumulator. This had to be carried, every so often, to be recharged in the distant village.

Food such as fresh eggs, milk, butter, and meat, could be purchased from some of the local farmers, who did not ask for Ration Coupons. But, to buy other types of foodstuffs, there was the long walk to the single village shop, and then back to the house, carrying your purchases. Your Ration Books had to be presented to the shopkeeper, and the relevant Ration Coupons extracted in order to obtain the limited food supplies that you were allowed to purchase.

2

But the boy loved it here; how exciting it was to survive in this natural, but difficult environment, and how different to what he knew back home. There they had mains water, gas, electricity, and an internal bathroom with an inside lavatory. He even had a small wind-up record player for entertainment, and his father had a top-of-the-range, mains Ekco valve wireless that could even pick up Paris, Berlin, and Radio Luxembourg.

But their large house had only open coal fires, for use in the winter, to warm its spacious rooms. So, when he went to bed, he had to snuggle deep down under his blankets and eiderdown, just to keep warm. In the morning, he did not get up, until his mother came into his room, to wake him for school. At the weekends, his mother came in to set and light a fire in his grate. At least, he then had a little warmth to get up, or stay in his room to read, if it was not good enough weather to go outside.

Part of his grandmother's front garden was a large Rock Garden; in it there were miniature lakes and rivers that he could dam, and he could float miniature boats and twigs from one tiny lake to another. Rather than walking up the hill of the sweeping drive, to get back to the house, there was a rocky cliff he could climb. He loved climbing this, despite the danger of falling. He soon got to know the best route up, and he used to practice this route and then race himself, using the second hand of his watch, to achieve the fastest ascent.

There was a secret trail, which he kept to himself, through the upper garden that came out on to a neighbouring farmer's field. He could walk, from there, over other fields. He was not scared of the cattle, or other livestock, that sometimes inhabited them. Then, of course, there was the route all the way up the back garden, to the highest point, where he could sit and take in the full magnificent views.

Then there was the sea; just two small fields away was a large expanse of rocky beach which, when the tide was out, turned into miles of sand. As the sea left, it exposed many pools full of sea creatures, and mounds of seaweed, all to explore. The sand was firm but, in places, was still cut through with rivulets of salt water. You could walk around the headland, even if the tide was fully in, and into the next bay, if you wanted to.

But it was important to always be aware of the tides. If you ventured far enough at low tide and did not mind getting your feet wet, there were some small islands which, at high tide, were surrounded by the sea. He had once persuaded his mother to carry a picnic to one of them. They had enjoyed themselves, watching the tide come in and experiencing the feeling of being alone, on their own isolated island, as they ate their picnic. But, she had made him promise, never to do this again, by himself, before the tide had ebbed and they could then return to the house.

He even had his own route to walk to the village; rather than walk down the narrow lanes, he walked along the pebbled beach in one particular direction, until he arrived at a small dam which controlled part of the tidal flow into an inlet. There was a narrow path along the top of this dam which continued, along a wooded country path, to the village. He used to visit the single village shop to buy his sweets ration and, if a train came by, watch it roaring through the small station. If it stopped, he watched the passengers who alighted, or got on to the train.

His one friend here was an older local farmer's son; at harvest time, they used to help gather and stack the hay on to a great haystack or, if they could catch it, joyously ride bareback on his father's horse which was kept to draw the plough, or pull the farm carts. The farmer's son told him stories about the animals on his father's farm, and about the wild animals that lived in the fields around the farm too. This wildlife abounded: hares, rabbits, foxes, red squirrels, and badgers could all be spotted. There was a particular red squirrel which came to play in the upper garden, and which his grandmother regularly fed with some scraps.

But his grandmother also loved the wild birds and prepared a special gruel for them made from stale bread marinated with water. She distributed this, in the garden, each morning and late afternoon, and also hung-up containers of it from the branches of some of the trees. These containers were placed so that they could easily watch the birds feeding from the windows of the house. Blackbirds, robins, thrush, tits, and chaffinches came and clung on to these containers full of this gruel, in order to feed. But his grandmother hated the magpies, which came to try and steal the feed from the other birds. She always clapped her hands and shouted to scare them away. Strangely, the seabirds did not seem interested in this feast; they merely flew high above and out, towards the sea, to catch their fish suppers.

3

Then there were also the great metal birds. Not far away was a Royal Air Force aerodrome where pilots were trained to fly jet fighters. Regularly, single Vampire training aircraft came roaring overhead or, sometimes, even two or three in formation. An old Gloster Meteor also put in an appearance, with its powerful, twin jet engines shaking the house and frightening away any feeding birds. Occasionally, the man lent the boy his old Royal Navy binoculars so that he could watch the aeroplanes, particularly if they were on a large circular course around the sky.

For the boy, this man was a source of fascinating stories and interest. He had served in the Royal Navy for many years, and had visited the Far East and many other different parts of the world. He had also taken part in some of the naval battles of the First World War. Sometimes, he used to lay out, in the lower garden, a large White Ensign, which he had been given from the last warship on which he had served. When he did this, the boy swore that he saw the fighter planes flying overhead, dip their wings, in salute. When outside, the man always wore his old Royal Navy cap and, too young to call him by his real name, the boy called him by the nickname he had made up for him. It was, appropriately, "Cap."

From this man, the boy heard many tales of far-away places, of the sea, and about life in the Royal Navy. He told him stories of the Orient, of China, Hong Kong, Burma, and Ceylon. Then there were tales about his visits to the strange world of Japan at the very beginning of the 20th century. He spoke about the warships he had served on, and about the friendship of his companions. But he never talked about the great sea battles that he had taken part in; the boy did not understand why, until he had grown up and had begun to understand more about the true horrors of war.

Sometimes, the old sailor would take out some large albums, hidden away in secret cupboards in the house or, from his workshop, in one of the wooden outbuildings. Then he would show the boy some old photographs of warships or of strange, distant places. Sometimes, he would find a mysterious object, made far away, and tell the boy the story of what it was and how it had been made in a distant land. Then, in other albums, were this man's collection of Post Cards, purchased in many different parts of the world. To each object, he always seemed to be able to attach a story, and the boy sat spell-bound and listened to them all.

When the boy came for his Easter holidays, the gorse bushes around the house were always in bloom; while not to be touched because of its sharp thorns, the blossoms of the gorse were an iridescent, bright yellow hue. The birds sang and the flowers bloomed, as all Nature awoke from its winter's slumbering. But the boy visited in winter too and had spent several Christmas holidays there. Rarely did they have snow, but it rained, and the great gales swept in from the Irish Sea. On those days, the whole house rattled from the high winds, and, on the nearby shore, the high tide lashed against the rocks.

When he could not go out, he sat in the large porch that the man had constructed all by himself, at the front of the house. It overlooked the sea and the great bulk of Holyhead Mountain. He had usually brought some books to read; his favourites were the "Just William" series by Richmal Crompton. Between pages, sitting there in the porch, every so often he used to glance up, to make sure that this wild view, had not changed. When it became too dark to read, he used to sit in the light of the oil lamps, and listen to the wireless.

It was important to hear the news on the wireless, but what was happening in London, or elsewhere in the country, seemed so far away as to be almost on another planet. He remembered, vividly, the news coming through that the King had died, and that they now had a new Queen called Elizabeth. Then, every evening, his grandmother would listen to "The Archers," an everyday story of farming life and country folk. After that, for the boy, it was almost time to go to bed. Soon, it was the same for the adults too, so as to save on the precious oil for the lamps.

Perhaps to remind her son of this wild and beautiful place, his mother had bought him a picture for his bedroom wall, back home in Shropshire. It was a fine print of a picture called "Sea Dreams," by the female French artist Marie Lucas-Robiquet. She had painted it in about 1930 when she was living on the Cote d'Azur. It was probably painted in Saint Tropez when it was still a small, undeveloped, fishing village. The picture showed a young boy, in ragged clothes, in front of the sea. To one side, was part of a ruined castle, on top of some low cliffs. The boy's gaze is not set upon the sea, but towards the artist. But he does not really see the artist, he is looking into the distance as he dreams, perhaps, of the far-away places that he could sail to, unhindered, on the vast ocean behind him.

4

The boy was still too young to understand the adult world. He did not query why his maternal grandmother lived so far away, from his maternal grandfather? He still lived back in Shropshire. He did not query why his grandmother, now lived with this other man? He only had one set of grandparents; both his father's parents had died long before he had been born.

He did not know, then, the story that his mother would later tell him, when he was old enough to understand. How her own mother had written to her, on her honeymoon in the South of France, to tell her that she had moved out of the house that his mother had been brought up in, and had run away to live with this other man in this isolated, but beautiful, place.

At the time, she had not told her own daughter where she had gone and, had warned her, that she should never try to find her. Years later, but still before the boy had been born, another letter had arrived for his future mother, via her mother's bank manager. This had promised to tell his mother, where her own mother now lived. But only if she solemnly promised, by writing back, via the bank manager, never to reveal the location to her own father!

So, the promise had been solemnly made; but it had clearly put a psychological strain on his future mother, who still loved both her parents, and also on her husband, his father. At last, a letter had arrived bearing his grandmother's address, with an invitation to visit. It had been with great difficulty that, on their first visit, the boy's father had been able to find his way to drive to this isolated house, which his wife's mother had secretly bought for herself and her lover.

Meanwhile, his mother's father had, in total disgust, sold the large house, which had been his daughter's childhood home. He had sold, as well, all its contents, including many family treasures, and his large collection of fine Coalport China. He had then spent most of his money by moving into a local hotel, as a permanent guest, for the rest of his life. He had complained bitterly about what his wife had done, but had never tried to divorce her. He was locally a prominent man, and rather wanted to live his public life, unblemished, and to totally forget the private life, that he had once had.

SEA DREAMS

He had already stood as an independent local Councillor, and was the senior Justice of the Peace for the ancient Borough, which then covered a large area of the southern part of the county. When he was elected Mayor of this Borough, he considered it a great honour, and asked his daughter to act as his Mayoress, which she gladly agreed to do. But neither she, nor her husband, ever revealed to him where his wife of over twenty-five years was now living, and who she was living with. Perhaps, in the end, he just did not care, and by now, did not even want to know.

As the boy slowly grew older, he began to learn more about the afflictions that always seem to burden human beings. His grandmother began to suffer from serious leg ulcers that would not heal. His grandfather had a major stroke, and then had died a few days later. His grandmother's lover took to his bed and died. In both cases, he was deemed to be still too young, to attend the funerals. His grandmother was left in her remote house; she refused to sell it and move out. Perhaps, she just wanted to remain, to help her remember the happy years that she had spent there. At last, she was connected to the electricity supply and then, even mains water and sewerage pipes, were brought to the house. Then, wonders of wonders, a telephone was installed so that his mother could speak to her mother whenever she wanted to, and make sure that she was alright.

But his grandmother was still very isolated and began to fear for her safety. Her lover had, years before, been issued with a small automatic pistol to protect himself when he went, as a Royal Navy officer, on shore leave in distant cities. He had always kept it in working order to shoot the rats that, sometimes, plagued the house's outbuildings. He had taught her how to shoot it and now she slept with it, loaded, under her pillow. It became a family joke that "Granny always sleeps with a loaded gun under her pillow!"

Eventually, she was taken into hospital and he visited her with his mother; he always remembered the smile with which she greeted her only grandchild. Then she had peacefully passed away; this time he was allowed to attend the funeral. His grandmother was buried in the same grave as her lover, in the small churchyard of a tiny, remote church, on the island that she loved. As her wild birds would have flown, it was just one mile away from her isolated house that the boy would always continue to remember, and where he had spent so many happy days of his childhood.

FINE WEATHER AND A FAIR WIND

"So we beat on, boats against the current, borne back ceaselessly into the past." – the last sentence of *The Great Gatsby* by F. Scott Fitzgerald.

1

The boy lay in his bed, with his face to the wall. He was looking at the picture, as he lay on his left-hand side. It was a fine, signed print by Montague Dawson, of a sailing yacht swiftly under way off the shore of some distant cliffs. The sea was calm, the sky blue, and its large sail was filled with wind. The picture was a present for his bedroom wall, from his mother. On the back of the frame was a label which gave the title of the picture; it was called "Fine Weather and a Fair Wind." He loved the sea and it had become his "Worry Picture." Whenever he was concerned about anything, he would feel immediately calmed by the vision of this great sea and the yacht speeding over it.

His bedroom walls were decorated with a light blue paint and, on the other side of his bed, was his desk. Because of the lack of materials in the second half of the 1940's, it had been made by a carpenter, simply, from two wooden orange boxes and a piece of wood attached between them. It was painted a much darker blue. Above his desk was a World Map from the same time; about one third of the world was coloured a dark pink. These were the many countries that were still then contained within the British Empire.

He was an only child, and lived with his parents in a small, Shropshire market town. He had lived there ever since he had been born and now he was nearly twelve years old. His home was a large, detached Victorian house, with five bedrooms. Downstairs, there was a sitting room and a dining room, which both faced the main road. At the back there was a large kitchen and a bright morning room, with French windows, looking out on to a long lawn. The house was heated with coal fires in each room, and the coal was stored in an outhouse in the garden and brought into the house, as and when it was needed.

At the end of the long garden was a large garage, for his father's car, and double gates that led out, via a short lane, to a side street. Originally, this garage block had housed a stable, and storage for several horse-drawn carriages. Above it were living quarters for a coachman and his family, with one large main room, which his parents now used to hold his annual birthday parties. The boy had acquired a tricycle when he was about six years old. Behind it, with a leather strap, he had attached a wooden truck on four wheels. He pretended that this was a lorry, like the large ones he saw on the main road, passing his house. He furiously rode his tricycle, with the truck behind it, around the garden, lap after lap after lap!

It was a settled existence and he now attended the local Church of England Primary School, just a short walk away. But this was not his first school, that had been a fee-paying preparatory school on the other side of the town. It was run by a strict Headmistress who also owned the school, and the boy had fallen out with her in his own childlike way. The problem was that he was naturally left-handed, and she insisted that he must learn to write with his right hand, like all her other pupils!

So the Headmistress had brought him home one afternoon, in a taxi. She had told his mother that she could do nothing with him. He was just too much trouble in class! He had then been transferred to the nearby Church of England school, which he had enjoyed. At least, there, they did not try and force him to write with his right hand! But soon he would move to the local boys Grammar School in the town, as he had recently taken and passed his Eleven Plus examination. That secondary school had been founded three hundred years before, and was known to offer its all-male pupils, a truly excellent education.

He only had a few friends, although he enjoyed his solitary status as an only child. He had found that reading, and his vivid imagination, was all that he needed. When he was younger, he had invented a whole new planet, orbiting a star in a distant galaxy, to inhabit and write about of his own. He wrote about it copiously, about its various lands, its peoples, and its government. His mother had got quite worried about all this but, then she had realised, that maybe he was just showing some talent for imagination and literary invention.

As an alternative to reading, he would listen to his father's black Ekco valve wireless, particularly in the evenings. There were some series that he loved listening to such as the B.B.C. series "Journey into Space," and "Riders of the Range," and on Radio Luxemburg, "The Ovaltineys". At the weekends, he usually played card games like "Happy Families," or "Snap," with his parents. In the holidays, he was taken, usually by his mother as his father had limited holidays at the bank where he worked, to stay with his maternal grandmother. She had an isolated house by the sea, on the island of Anglesey. There he could explore the beauty of the surrounding area and enjoy his solitary walks.

They ate well at home. Food Rationing had finally finished the previous year, but he still recalled shopping with his mother in the long High Street of the town, when any food shopping had to be accompanied by the inevitable Ration Book, and the individual food coupons being extracted from it by each shopkeeper. His mother did not pay, of course, unless it was for a small item like a newspaper or a loaf of bread. Instead, an account was kept by the butcher, the greengrocer, and the other shops, and his father used to pay their accumulated bills on a monthly basis. Also, his mother only used to carry light items of shopping home; all the rest of the groceries were delivered to the house.

At the weekends, they used to take the train on the little branch line from the town's station, just up the road. Their visits were usually to the county town of Shrewsbury, where he could find various toy shops, attend a film, or have a meal in a restaurant with his parents. If it was a fine day, a walk in the Quarry Park, alongside the River Severn, was the usual pastime. In the middle of the Quarry Park was the large hollow known as The Dingle, which, in the Spring and Summer, was resplendent with a wonderful variety of flowers. There were also ducks and other water birds, with their chicks, to see on its lake.

His father's parents were long dead but his maternal grandfather was still alive; he lived less than twenty miles away. They visited him from time to time, in the hotel where he now permanently lived. Occasionally, he would hire a car and driver to visit them for lunch at the weekend. The boy never queried why his grandfather lived in a hotel, so far from his grandmother, and why his grandmother lived in her isolated house in North Wales, with another man?

His grandfather was a prominent man in the civic affairs of the ancient Borough, where he lived. He had many friends, including the Lord Lieutenant of the County. He was both a local Councillor and a Justice of the Peace. It was no surprise, therefore, when he was elected Mayor of his ancient Borough. Having no available wife, he invited his daughter, the boy's mother, to become his Mayoress. She loyally fulfilled this role for her father, carrying out her duties as required, sometimes accompanied by her small son, to the numerous events and ceremonies.

When they had to entertain at home, the boy's parents did it in style; a cook and a maid were recruited locally for the occasion, so that his mother would not be too over-stretched with the work to be done, and could act as the charming hostess. If his mother wanted to visit any of her friends, or had an official function to attend, the boy was looked after by his Nanny, a married woman without children who lived locally. His mother was used to having staff and had never learnt to dress herself until after her marriage. At her childhood home she had always had her own maid to help dress and undress her. Meanwhile, his father never touched the large garden. Instead, a gardener was recruited and attended to the work to be done in the garden for a couple of days a week, when necessary.

The boy remembered also that, when he was younger, they had had a live-in maid. Every morning, she used to wake him with a cheery "Good Morning!" She had come to light the coal fire in his bedroom grate, which she had laid the evening before. In winter, this fire would take its time to warm even a small part of his large bedroom. But now the maid had left and there was no longer a coal fire in the winter mornings. He had to crawl reluctantly out of bed, in order to get dressed as quickly as he could, in the freezing cold room.

2

The boy was now feeling uncertain, but he did not know why. A few days before, a strange event had occurred. It had been, in some ways, exciting. He and his mother had been picked up, in the long High Street, by a man in a large, luxury car, who had obviously spotted them as they were walking back from some shopping. He had been introduced to the man who he had remembered meeting before; he was the owner of a large brewery in a neighbouring town, and he knew him to be a friend of his grandfather.

He had been put into the back of the large car and his mother had sat in the front, with the driver. The man had parked his luxury car in a side road, so as not to attract too much attention, then the two adults had talked very quietly together. He could not hear what was being said; even if he had been able to hear, he would probably not have understood it. But he saw that his mother became upset and had started crying about what the man was telling her. After about an hour, the man had delivered them both back to their house, and had then driven quickly away.

Over the coming days, he had sensed a change of attitude between his parents. He had heard them arguing at night, after he had gone to bed. The routine of the house began to change; his father did not seem to return from work as early as he used to. When his parents were together, he observed that there was a silence between them. His mother had become even more loving to him. She took him out for some treats and, at the weekends, on a trip by train to the county town. But his father did not now accompany them.

Several times he found his mother sitting by herself, in her bedroom, crying. "It is nothing, dear," she would say if he asked her, "What was the matter?" Soon he started at his new school, and the excitement of moving there made him forget his worries for a while. There were new friends to make, although some of the boys had moved with him from his local primary school. There were new schoolmasters to get to know, and new subjects to start to study.

His first two terms at his new school went well, but he could not shake off his sense of unease. One Saturday, his mother had taken him, by the local train, to Shrewsbury where they went for a walk in the Quarry Park. They had been chatting about some normal things, and then, there were a few minutes of silence. She turned to him and tried to find the words.

"I have something to tell you, dear," she said. "At the end of your school year, we are going to move away. You will have to start again at another new school."

"Why is that?" he asked, rather put off by this sudden news and the thought of so many changes.

She paused, and then said bitterly, "It is your father's fault." The story then came tumbling out of her. "Your father is going to have to leave his job at the bank. He has been very silly and has lost all his money. Then he borrowed some more money, from some customers of the bank, and lost that too. We will have to sell the house, to pay off what he owes the bank on the mortgage on our house. He will then have to pay back what he has borrowed from these other people. The bank has said that they do not want him to work for them anymore. We will have to use what money we have left, to move away, because of the disgrace that your father has caused. But your father thinks that we will move to a place where he might be able to find a new job. There we will have to rent a flat, because we will not have enough money to buy a new house."

He was silent for a few minutes in order to digest this news. "But how did he lose his money, Mummy?" he asked.

"Gambling on horse races," replied his mother. "I knew nothing about what he was doing, until I was told by a friend of your grandfather's, who had found out what was happening."

"But why did he do this, Mummy?" the boy asked.

"I really do not know, dear," his mother replied. "But some people just get addicted to gambling, and your father always did gamble, but only in a small way. Perhaps he would put a small bet on a horse, if we both went to a Point-to-Point race meeting. Then, when he was younger, he told me that he used to gamble when playing card games with his friends. But that was nothing like this. I cannot understand what happened to make him gamble away so much of our money!"

So it came to pass. By the beginning of his third term at his new school, obvious preparations were being made to move away from the town in which he had been born. His mother had obtained a large number of tea chests, packing cases, and cardboard boxes; these she slowly filled with the various ornaments, crockery, and pictures in the house. Each item was carefully wrapped in newspaper and placed carefully in their container so that, hopefully, it would not be damaged. The end of his third term came; a special Fair was held at his school to celebrate the fact that it had been founded exactly three hundred years before. It was the very last event that he would attend there.

3

Soon, they were ready to move. Their furniture was taken away to be sold, except for a few pieces that his Mother wanted to keep. Their furniture would not be needed as they would now be living in a furnished flat. Then the removal van arrived one morning, to take away the rest of their possessions. His father had to sell his car, as he could no longer afford to keep it running. So, once the removal van had left, they had to set out on the long train journey down to the small South Wales coastal resort of Tenby, where his father had decided that they should now live. He had found a job there; it was as a door-to-door salesman selling sets of encyclopaedias. His income would now depend, only, on what he could sell!

The journey took hours, with two changes of trains, and they arrived late and tired at their new home. It was an apartment overlooking the sea and a sandy beach. There was an outside veranda, with fine sea views, and a long flight of steep steps down to the beach. The boy became excited about his new home, and soon he would start to attend the local Grammar School. He was a little concerned about this; he had heard that there would be girls at his new school, as well as boys. Unfortunately, he had got used to a boys-only education, so girls were now something that he would have to get used to!

After a few months, they had settled, and the boy was beginning to enjoy his new school. The only strange thing was the furniture around them, which he could not get used to because it was not their own. The furniture included a pianola with a collection of long paper rolls, perforated with holes, which played the piano automatically if you wound up a clockwork mechanism inside it. As his father had sold his wireless, for entertainment in the evenings, they used to take out several of these paper rolls to hear the tunes being played. The only problem was that the paper rolls played only hymns from the Ancient and Modern Hymns collection!

After a while, his mother had a quiet word with his father, and they used some of the money that they still had left, to buy a new, small, black and white television set. The boy was very excited about this; for the first time they would have some real entertainment in the long evenings. It involved an aerial being fixed, by the man who delivered the television, to the outside veranda. For this work to be done of course, they had to get the flat owner's permission. Then the man turned the television on to adjust it and, for the first time, the boy saw the small, black and white, glowing, flickering screen.

His father had been trying to find a new, proper job, but it proved very difficult as his former bank refused to give him a reference. In the end, he just had to take only what was on offer. To the sale of sets of encyclopaedias, he managed to add the published works of the still popular war-time Prime Minister, Sir Winston Churchill. Because he did not want to become known for doing this type of work in the small town in which they now lived, his father travelled far and wide, in the surrounding area, to try and make a paltry living. But it was very difficult to make money, and he had to spend money on travel, just to reach where he wanted to try and sell these books. Soon, they could not afford the rent of their seaside apartment anymore, and had to move to a cheaper flat.

By now all his parents' savings had run out, and soon they had to move again. After several such moves, they ended up living in one sparsely furnished room together. His father refused to approach the Social Services; he was too proud a man to do that. After all, it was his fault that he had brought himself and his family to this state and neither he, nor the boy's mother, could see why the taxpayer should now have to pay to help them out.

Then his father decided that he could, perhaps, make more money by moving to an area with a larger population. So he moved his family again, this time to a small town on the outskirts of Cardiff. But, for some reason, this did not work out for him either and, after just a few months there, they moved once again, this time to Swansea. By now, the boy had experienced three changes of secondary schools, and his education was beginning to suffer. With so little money, they had to cut down on buying food, and they lived a Spartan existence, eating only the most basic of food to keep alive. There was no money for new clothes, and his Mother was always trying to patch and mend the few clothes that they had.

Nor was there any money for holidays or to travel; his long summer holidays at his grandmother's house in North Wales, had been stopped. He began to experience some psychosomatic symptoms, and complained of pains in his legs that stopped him from walking properly and, of course, from attending school. The doctor, that his worried parents had called, could find nothing physically wrong, but he agreed that the boy should be kept away from school.

Tiring of the struggle to make sufficient money this way, his father decided to change his work. Ever optimistic, he decided to take on selling Football Pools, now going door-to-door to collect bets, every week, from people gambling small amounts on the results of football matches to be played the following Saturday. He managed to earn a small commission from doing this work, but the company that ran the business told him that he had better prospects of making money in the North-West of England, rather than in Wales. So he again moved his family, back to England, to Southport in Lancashire.

By now the boy was exhausted and depressed; he was tired of moving around the country, and of being unable to get a proper education. He had noticed that the relationship between his parents had soured even further, with occasional physical aggression and threats made on his mother, by his father. The boy was now of the age to be able to persuade his mother to do something about this situation and so he quietly began to discuss with her the need to leave his father and move away to a stable home, in a place where he could get a proper education.

Fortunately, his mother had been personally granted a small income from a Charity Fund belonging to the bank that had previously employed his father. This had only happened because of his grandfather's connections; he had written to the Chairman of the bank to ask for some financial help for his daughter. After all, his son-in-law had paid money over many years, into the bank's Pension Fund, and the bank was now denying him any pension.

With this small amount of money, they both left his father. His mother decided to move back to Swansea, where she had made some friends. They found a house, which they could share, with a kindly lady who owned it. His mother applied for her son to go back to his former Grammar school where he had been for only two school terms, having missed many months of this schooling because of his illness. But he had, by now, lost so much of his education, that the Local Authority decided to place him in a new Comprehensive school where he would have to repeat a whole year of his schooling in order to catch up.

4

Once settled in, he worked ferociously hard at his new school. He was determined to try and rescue his education, and to show his mother that he could be a success. A number of his new teachers noticed this determination, and tried to help him. One of them, his English master, was unconventional and encouraged the boys to read widely. One day, in class, he told them about a new writer they should try and read: his name was Ian Fleming and he wrote about a spy called James Bond.

A school trip was planned to the National Museum of Wales in Cardiff, for some of the older boys. Their English teacher told them that their visit to Cardiff would coincide with the publication, in paperback, of a great book by the writer D. H. Lawrence. This book had been banned up to now, but a recent Court case had, at last, allowed its publication. It was called "Lady Chatterley's Lover". So it was that a whole number of the boys, who maybe looked older than their years, had managed to purchase a copy of this famous book at a large book shop in Cardiff, during their time off for shopping after their museum visit. On the coach back home, these numerous copies were handed around the coach, and the best, and the most sexually revealing parts of the book, had been quickly identified!

The boy blossomed at his new school; in his second year he was made a Prefect and, at the end of that school year, he took his General Certificate of Education, Ordinary Level examinations. Then it was a Pass or Fail decision, and the Pass Rate was set high. He managed a Pass in nine subjects including English, Mathematics, Physics, and Chemistry. Still ambitious, he entered the Sixth Form where he would study Mathematics, Physics, and Chemistry, with the aim of applying to University to study for a Science Degree.

But it was not to be; his mother was finding life very difficult. Desperate for money, and really too proud to claim any social benefits, she had to find a job. She had not worked since her teenage years when, after she had left her private school, she had found a job in a first-class, ladies' clothes shop in Shrewsbury. When she married, like many other middle-class women of that time, she had become a full-time housewife.

With her good looks and refined manners, she found work in the cocktail bar of a privately-owned hotel and country club. Here she was able to talk to the guests, on an equal basis. But the wife of the hotel owner became jealous. This barmaid was taking attention away from her, as the owner's wife, so that job did not last long. Her next employment was at a bigger seaside hotel, in the same role, and as well as a salary, she was given accommodation. She found her son a room in a house just across the road from this hotel, owned by two old sisters. She tried to see him whenever she could spare the time from trying to earn some money. But, again, this job did not last long, and she had to plead with the two old sisters to be allowed to move into her son's room, to sleep on a uncomfortable camp bed.

Her son began to find this situation impossible; they were now so poor that they could hardly afford to eat. "I will have to find a job, Mother," he said to her one day. "We cannot go on like this anymore. I must go out and earn some money." So he made his own decision to leave school, and through their local branch, he applied for a job at his father's old bank. A letter arrived for him, enclosing a Travel Warrant that he could exchange for a train ticket. He was to report two weeks later, for an interview, at the Head Office of the bank, in London.

With the last of her small savings, his mother bought him a smart, two-piece suit, a white shirt, a sober tie, and some black shoes. On the appointed day, he set out to catch an early bus to the station, and then an express train to London. He had only a small amount of money in his pocket, which his mother had given him. When he arrived he was overawed with London; the crowds, the smells, and the noise were something that he had never experienced before. Carefully, he negotiated the London

Underground system, and arrived at the bank's Lombard Street Head Office in good time.

The building was huge and impressive and long, high, polished, wooden counters with polished brass fittings, occupied the central space. There were numerous, manned, cashier's positions, and clerks sitting behind them with calculating machines, or writing in thick ledgers. In the middle of the floor of the public space, was a large mosaic of a Black Horse, the symbol of the bank. The building spoke loudly about the status and solidity of this banking institution. He timidly asked one of the cashiers what he should do, and was told to sit and wait on some chairs drawn up against a wall. Soon he was collected by a smartly dressed lady, and taken upstairs. There, again, he sat and waited, until he was called into a small office.

In the office, he was interviewed by a kindly, man, who had a file in front of him. He asked some questions, which the boy managed shyly to answer. Then the man said, "You have done well at school." The man then consulted his file again, and said what the boy was dreading! "I see that your father worked for us, for some years."

The embarrassed boy managed to stammer out; "Yes, he did, sir. But he retired from the bank early."

FINE WEATHER AND A FAIR WIND

The interview over he left the bank, realising that he was now hungry. He found a cheap sandwich bar and sat inside, watching the hurrying crowds of people, here, in the City of London, the very centre of financial power. He had not been told if he had a job, and worried that his father's bad record with the bank would come back to haunt him. He found his way back to Paddington Station, and then took the train back to Swansea.

One week later, a letter arrived: he was asked to report, at ten o'clock in the morning, a week the following Monday, at a branch of the bank in a nearby town. His small salary and other conditions were detailed in an attached appendix. He was asked to reply, by return, if he wished to accept the bank's offer of employment. He told his Mother, who was overjoyed. "We will soon be able to afford to rent our own flat now," he said to her. "And we will be able to buy some better food and clothes." So their hard struggle, against the adverse tides of life, had begun to abate, and they now hoped to look forward to perhaps again facing "Fine Weather and a Fair Wind."

THE NEW MAN

"Probus et Fidelis" (Honest and Trustworthy) – the motto of the Chartered Institute of Bankers.

1

The sparks flew up from the hot fire; he had the heavy iron door open, and was shovelling more fuel into the furnace. He was using the large old spade provided, to recharge the boiler from the great pile of coal in the branch's outhouse. Edwards had taken off his jacket and tie as he did not want any of the red-hot cinders to burn a hole in his new suit. But this did not protect either his trousers, or his new white shirt, from the glowing embers. He had really not expected to have to do this. But it was a Saturday morning, and his branch of the bank was open. The Caretaker always had every Saturday off and, as the most junior male member of staff present that morning, he was expected to replace the Caretaker in the task of keeping the central heating system going for this branch, on a cold winter's day.

His other regular tasks included replacing worn-out nibs on the pens, which had been put out on the counters for the use of customers, and filling the many ink wells provided. In addition, he had to replace the used sheets of blotting paper contained in the smart leather holders, also provided for the customer's use, on the branch's counters and tables in the public area of the branch.

It was October 1961 and just two weeks before, Edwards had reported to this branch of the bank, as requested, promptly, at ten o'clock in the morning.. It was to be his first morning, after leaving school, in the adult world of work. Over two years before, he and his Mother had left his Father to try and stabilise their lives, and for Edwards to properly finish his school education. His Father had lost his job, after some thirty years in the same bank, because his heavy gambling habit had been discovered and the fact that he had borrowed money from some of the bank's customers to fuel it.

It had been a long, financial struggle to survive, and he now felt that he must work, to earn some money to help support himself and his mother. For his job interview in London he had worn his smart, new suit that his mother had bought for him, with the last of her savings, along with a clean, white shirt and a sober tie. This morning, he was wearing the some clothes again and his black leather shoes gleamed from the polishing that he had given them the previous night. He had to start off early; he first had a long bus journey to the railway station and then a short train journey to this, his first place of work.

The branch was located in a large town to the east of Swansea. The building itself was large and impressive and he felt somewhat dwarfed as he entered it. He identified himself at one of the cashier's positions, and was then shown through the solid wooden door into the large office space that lay behind the line of polished oak counters. He was taken by a young lady, in a light blue overall, to meet the Chief Clerk. He sat in his own imposing, raised wooden enclosure, so that he could keep a steely eye on all the clerks and lady machinists working around him. Edwards was surprised by the warmth of the welcome that this man gave him, and he passed over, as requested, the letter that he had received asking him to report at this time and place.

"To start with," the Chief Clerk promptly told him, "you will report to this young lady. She will teach you to use an adding machine, and also acquaint you with your duties as the Office Junior."

It took Edwards some time to learn the foibles of the adding machine, although the young lady, whose name was Carol, was a very good teacher. She then sent him on a regular journey, to gather what she called the "Waste," from the wooden boxes behind each cashier's position. For security, the cashiers were locked into their own special area. But periodically, they reached back, to deposit the wads of cheques and paying-in slips that they had collected from their customers, into their respective box.

Then Carol showed him how to sort the "Waste" into a logical sequence; pairing cheques with paying-in slips and, having explained the simple basics of double-entry bookkeeping, she showed him how to enter the amount of each item on the adding machine. The machine then produced a long role of printed figures, the totals of which had to be checked and then entered, by hand, into the appropriate columns on the "Waste Sheet" for that day. Finally, came the day when he was allowed to operate the machine himself. He nervously picked up a pen in one hand. "Don't do that!" said Carol sharply. "Leave both of your hands completely free to do the work."

For four weeks, Carol supervised him and, only when she was satisfied that he was now fully competent, did she take him over to the "Posting Pool." Here, a number of other young ladies, all in their requisite light blue overalls, entered each Debit and Credit item on the appropriate Ledger Sheet for each customer who had a Current Account at that branch. The loose-leaf Ledger Sheets were kept in large metal containers, filed in strict alphabetical order. The machines, used to "Post" or enter each item, were large and complicated. It took Edwards weeks to learn how they worked, and his processing rate always remained low.

Here, he was taught by Lorna, a dark eyed and dark-haired beauty and sometimes, he had to admit to himself, he found it difficult to concentrate on what she was telling him! The girls in the "Posting Pool" laughed and joked with him or, maybe, at him. He was never really quite sure as his experience with young women, so far, had been minimal, and sometimes he felt himself blushing with embarrassment!

After some six weeks of this exacting and painstaking work, he was considered by Lorna to understand fully the task and had reached the right level of competence for, what was involved, in this part of the work of a bank branch. His next job of work was to learn how to deal with the Deposit and Savings Accounts, where bank customers could keep their surplus funds. The Savings Section was mainly for small deposits, and often the accounts were in the name of children, opened by their parents. But both types of accounts were kept in large, heavy ledgers, and amounts paid in and drawn out, along with the calculation of interest, were entered by means of a pen and ink. This time he was supervised by a man, who seemed to Edwards to be old, although he was probably no more than thirty!

He was taught, first, to make entries on spare pieces of paper, before being allowed to make an entry in the actual ledger. Only when he could make an ink entry neatly and clearly, without any mistakes, and without smudging the ink, was he even allowed to start "posting" entries from a pile of deposit and withdrawal slips. He found this work somewhat tedious although, in time, he sensed a certain satisfaction after he had achieved a number of easily read, clean, and neat ledger entries.

2

A Current Account had been opened at this branch in his own name, a few days after he had started to work there. He always remembered the thrill of seeing his first monthly salary being "Posted" into it by one of the girls using one of the big machines, and seeing the Ledger Sheet, marked in red: "Staff," with his name at the top. Up to then his mother had been providing him with the daily money for his bus and train fares, but now he could make out his own cheque, for cash, from the new cheque book he had been given, and ask one of the cashiers to cash it for him.

He had worked for some four weeks at the branch before, one afternoon, Edwards was called into the office of the Branch Manager, to meet him. He had seen this man occasionally walking around the branch, or consulting with his Chief Clerk, but of course, as the Office Junior, he felt that he could not speak to him unless he was spoken to first. The Manager had his own private office, with his Personal Secretary seated outside to type his letters and handle all his incoming correspondence. His office also had a door out into the public area of the bank so that he could, if needed, usher important customers directly into his room. He had, of course, a most respectable position in the town; he was a member of the local Golf Club and mixed with the other professionals such as the lawyers, accountants, and doctors, as well as with the local councillors and other note-worthies of the town.

Edwards experienced some trepidation as he was shown, by his Personal Secretary, into the office of this exalted individual. But he was again greeted warmly. "You have been with us for a few weeks now," said his Branch Manager. "So, I thought that it was about time for us to meet. How are you getting on?"

"I think fine, sir. Thank you, sir." replied a nervous Edwards.

"Good," beamed his Manager. "But there is one thing that I must say to you. Even my wife knows absolutely nothing of what happens in this building. The affairs of this bank and its customers must never be discussed with any outsiders. I hope that you fully understand that and that you will always keep to that sacred rule." Edwards willingly agreed.

The cost of his travelling to this branch was high, both in time, and money. It therefore came as a pleasant surprise when he was told, after about six months into the job, that he would be transferred the following month to a branch actually in Swansea, which could be reached by a lot easier and cheaper journey from his home. Having said that, he had, by now, got to know the people in his first branch well and, as a result of his itinerant schooldays, he still found any change difficult to accept.

He settled slowly into his new smaller branch; the staff there were friendly, and he was immediately able to contribute because of the training that he had already been given. But the Manager always sets the atmosphere of each Branch, and this particular Manager seemed difficult. He was moody, and sometimes treated his staff in a totally offhand manner. Edwards found it difficult to understand what this man really wanted, and one morning he was called into his office. The Manager handed him a sheaf of papers, which included a Railway Warrant. "Head Office has decided that you must now attend the Beginner's Course at the Bank's Training Centre in Surrey," he said. "It lasts six weeks, which makes it difficult for me as we will have to cope without you!"

Despite his fear of change, Edwards was excited. For the first time, he would be away from home. But, when he told his mother that evening, she seemed worried. "We will have to buy you some more clothes," she said. "You will also need a trunk to put them in, to take with you."

"But think of all the saving on food, Mother," he said. "Everything is provided for me, once I get there." He sensed that his mother would be lonely without him but, then, he had taken on this job, and he was anxious to make the very best of it.

The day came, and he took an early bus to the train station, and then an express train to London. But, at Reading, Edwards got off the express as instructed, to take a branch line to a country station, where he was to be met. Outside the station, a coach was waiting to take him and the other young men, for they were all men, to the bank's Training Centre which occupied three very large country houses set on the edge of the Devil's Punch Bowl. This was, and still is, a wild area of land, which forms a very large natural depression in the surrounding Surrey countryside.

On arrival, they were each allocated a bed in a room with three other students, with communal bathroom facilities just down the corridor. Dining and communal leisure facilities, and some other bedrooms, were in an adjoining country house, and the classrooms and other training facilities were in a third, large residence, just down a country lane. Before dinner that evening, the Principal welcomed them to the Centre and explained the routine that they must now all follow. He then allocated them to their separate classes, each of which had some eight to ten students in the class.

The following morning, the course started in earnest. There were lessons on the rules and regulations of the bank, and they were given an idea on how to deal with the needs of customers, and the products that the bank could offer them. As well as classroom work, there was a large room with numerous machines of the type that Edwards was already familiar with. Because some branches were not supplied with such machines, zero knowledge was assumed, and Edwards was pleased that the careful training that he had already been given, gave him a head start in this type of work. At the end of every day they were given items to study in the evening and, the following morning, there was a written test on that homework, as well as some questions on previous items that they had been taught.

Two afternoons each week were given over to sport, carried out both in a gymnasium, or on the playing fields that surrounded the three large houses. They finished early every Friday to take part in a long run around the Devil's Punch Bowl. Edwards, unfortunately, did not like the sports; he had never been good at sport, partly because his body had been starved of proper nourishment during the long years since his father had been dismissed from his job at the bank. There had been such a shortage of money, that they really could not eat properly.

At the weekends, they were given permission to leave the Training Centre, as long as they returned, promptly, before the time set for dinner. A visit to the nearby town was possible, to shop or to watch a film, or perhaps to take a train for a longer trip away. One Saturday, Edwards took the train with some of his fellow students, up to London, to see some of the city's sights.

On another weekend, the same group took a train south to Portsmouth, for a visit to Nelson's famous flagship H.M.S. Victory. Edwards studied hard and soon was top of his class; while he failed to win in terms of sport, he could excel in the work and study required. At the end of the six week course, there were two days of extensive exams. Then they were allowed to relax with a day of gruelling, competitive races around, and in the depths of, the Devil's Punch Bowl!

At the end of that day, Edwards was exhausted. He struggled to his bed to rest, and nearly missed the last formal dinner of the course. Here, the Principal was due to give them their examination marks, and hand out some certificates of achievement. He just managed to make it to his table in time, which was now partly covered with the unusual sight of some wine bottles! Up to now, they had not been permitted to drink alcohol, but this was to be their farewell party. Then came the time for the examination results to be announced; only three students had failed to pass and they would be asked to take the course again.

The names of those who had passed were read out, but Edwards's name was not mentioned. He grew worried. The Principal paused dramatically. "Now for our leading students," he said. Third was a student whom Edwards shared a room with, the second most successful student was from another room. But the student who would be given the distinction of having passed with the highest marks on this course, was Edwards.

3

He returned home to his mother, and to continue his work at his branch of the bank. On his second morning back, his Manager called him into his room. He had a letter in front of him; it was obviously from the bank's Training Centre, with a report on Edwards. The Manager, for the first time, smiled at him. "You did exceptionally well on your course," he said. "I am very pleased with you, and you are a credit to me and to my branch." Edwards was pleased that his efforts had, at last, been recognised by this man.

"Thank you, sir," he responded.

"What are you going to do now, to further your career?" his Manager then asked Edwards.

"I was thinking, sir, of starting to study for the Institute of Bankers examinations," replied Edwards, who had already researched where he could carry out such study.

"An excellent idea," beamed his Manager.

So Edwards began his efforts to achieve this professional qualification that was available for him to take: a series of ten examination papers, in two parts, which would finally bring him the qualification of an Associate of the Chartered Institute of Bankers. He first had to apply to join the Institute, and pay the annual fee that was required. Then, every week, for two or three evenings a week, he did not return home until very late. Instead, after his full day of work at the bank, he took a bus to the local Technical College and sat in classrooms being taught in the subjects for these examinations. They covered mainly

Law, Economics, and Accountancy, and were well taught by experienced people in these disciplines.

At the weekends, he rigorously completed his homework, and the additional study required of him. After two years of study, he had passed the first five examinations, and then started on to the second, more difficult, part of the syllabus. The final examination, of Practice of Banking, brought in all the components of what he had learned, and also contained practical questions on how to deal with the affairs of both corporate and individual customers. It had a very high pass mark, and many students were known to fail this examination. But Edwards worked hard, as he had done during his last two years of school, to reach a final success. After four years of hard work, he finally qualified as an Associate of the Institute, probably one of the youngest bankers in the country to do so.

As he progressed, his Manager seemed to warm to him. One morning, he even came out of his office to present to Edwards, in front of his colleagues, the certificate that signified that he had successfully completed the first part of his examinations. "I will now promote you to a Cashier," he said. Edwards was thrilled; for nearly three years he had watched, from behind their positions, the work of the Cashiers who had daily face-to-face contact with the bank's customers.

THE NEW MAN

The morning came and for the first time, he was admitted to the secure area, immediately behind the bank's counters, where the money was kept. He was given his own till to manage, with a small amount of real money both in notes, and coins. He was carefully instructed by the Senior Cashier of the branch, who was a charming lady called Margaret, some ten years older than Edwards.

He was taught by Margaret, the most efficient way to keep his "Till" of notes and coins, and how he had to balance this cash amount against the amounts of all his transactions at the end of every day. Then he was shown how to lock up his "Till" in the branch's secure strong room, every night. He was also shown how to enter all his cash transactions, both in and out, in a long list on a printed "Cash Sheet." Then, as no adding machines were available, it was necessary to "cast," or add up, this long sheet of some sixty lines of figures, for each column of the sheet. A good Cashier should be able to add up this whole list of items, accurately, in his head, in just a few minutes!

At last he was allowed regular contact with the bank's customers, although for about a week, Margaret sat at his shoulder to introduce him to the regular customers, and to help him. Edwards, although still shy, was of a naturally sociable disposition, and he soon warmed to this new task. There were, of course, the regular business customers, mainly the shops and other businesses in the immediate area. They came in nearly every day to pay in their takings or, once a week, to draw out money to pay their staff. Then there were the personal customers; he was warned about the particular foibles of some of them by Margaret.

"This particular lady customer will always expect new banknotes when she comes in to cash her cheque," she told him. "Always keep a small amount of new banknotes for her."

Then he was told: "This particular shopkeeper will never fill in his paying in book himself. He always brings in his items, in a complete mess, and he expects you to sort it all out, and fill in all the figures for him."

He was taught how to count banknotes quickly and accurately, and how to bundle them up, in stated amounts, using the paper bands provided. Then he was shown how to count coins, and to parcel them up in paper bags in an appropriate total amount. Scales were available, with a set of weights provided, to check the weight of these bags to show that he had counted them accurately. From being always available as a "Third Cashier" to open his till position when the branch suddenly filled up with customers, he graduated to being a permanent "Second

Cashier", with a position next to Margaret, the Senior Cashier of the branch.

Gradually he got to know the regular customers, and they got to know him. Some of them started to choose him to come to, particularly if they were men and wanted to indulge in some light banter with this young man! Sometimes, customers of other branches would turn up, wanting to obtain some money by cashing their own cheque. If no prior arrangement had been made, this involved the Cashier requesting some form of identification, and then telephoning the particular branch involved to ascertain that this customer did have sufficient funds on their account to cash the cheque that he wanted.

One morning the local fishmonger arrived at Edwards's cashier's position. From a bag he took out a great wad of paper. "I found these under my counter," he said. "Can you do something with them?" They were a great wad of the old white Five Pound notes, and they were stuck together with age. Because of where they had been hidden, they stank of fish to High Heaven!

Edwards carefully separated them out and counted them. "We will have to send these to the Bank of England, sir," he told his customer. "They are no longer in circulation, but they will then credit us for their total amount, and we can then credit your account." Despite the disgusting smell, he knew that his duty was to be polite, to keep smiling, and to do everything that he could do to help this customer of the bank. After the man had left, he closed his cashier's position down to go to the staff bathroom and thoroughly wash his hands!

4

By now, Edwards was a trusted employee of the bank. As well as his own "Till" as a branch Cashier, which often contained several thousand Pounds, he was entrusted with the physical transfer of far larger sums of cash between his branch, and the major branch, where larger cash reserves were kept. These sums were either bank notes, surplus to requirements, or old and battered bank notes, taken out of circulation, and on their way to be burnt. In return, he collected new bank notes, to be introduced into circulation. The money was placed in a locked bag, chained around Edwards's waist. Edwards kept the key to the bag in his pocket and a taxi was ordered, from a trusted taxi firm, to transport him and his burden on a door-to-door basis.

Because of staff shortages, he was sometimes asked to take on the job of attending a sub-branch, away from his usual place of work. This involved taking a cash float in a bag, usually on public transport, to the sub-branch, and opening it up for customers to visit during its business hours. These hours were listed in a notice on its front door, which Edwards opened up with the keys provided to him.

Most of these sub-branches were up one of the Swansea Valleys where the single street of the town wound up the valley between steep hills, which were dotted with coal mines and spoil heaps. The sun rarely penetrated these valleys, and the air was permanently filled with the smell of coal dust. The customers, although they were always very friendly, looked at him as if he was some alien creature from another world which, indeed in many ways, he was.

He was now working on the last two examinations of his Institute of Bankers qualification, when he was moved to a larger branch. There his Manager seemed determined to try and help him. "I will give you the job to work as the Assistant to the Securities Clerk," he said. "In time, maybe, you will be able to replace him." The Securities Clerk was always the most technically qualified person in any branch; they were responsible for the safe custody of the stocks and shares certificates owned by the branch's customers, for their purchase and sale if required, and with looking after the locked metal boxes kept by some customers, in the branch's own Strong Room. That was where its cash reserves were also stored safely overnight.

In addition, the Securities Clerk was responsible for the legal work of taking security or collateral from customers, such as a mortgage over their property, to help secure a loan made to them. If asked, they also offered the service of completing and submitting, for a fee, a customer's annual Tax Return. It was overall a very skilled and responsible job, and it was unusual for someone of Edwards's young age to be asked to do it.

Edwards was thrilled; for the first time he was being asked to do some really challenging work, where he could apply some of the things that he had learnt from his banking studies. The Securities Clerk, who was much older than he was, showed him how to do a few things, but then left him to his own devices while he went off to do some other duties. Soon Edwards was interviewing important bank customers about their more complex needs, and dealing with their private business matters, as well as taking and "perfecting" the securities used to support the risk of loans advanced to customers. Then the news came through that he had passed his last two banking examinations; his Manager and his colleagues congratulated him warmly. He realised that he was now one of the youngest Associates of the Chartered Institute of Bankers in the country!

But where was his path onward from here? One of his colleagues had invited him home to meet his parents and, at dinner at their home that evening, his older brother had also been present. He now lived in London and was a Junior Lecturer in Economics at a College which was part of London University. Edwards had grown to be very interested in the subject of Economics and questioned him as to how, perhaps, he could, just out of interest, take a degree in that subject. "As you are a mature student, who has been working for five years, you should apply for a Leverhulme Scholarship," was the reply. So Edwards did!

A few months later, he received an invitation to attend an interview at the College. He took the time off as a holiday and travelled, by train, to London for the day. He was expecting an interview similar to that he had experienced for his banking job: a one-to-one across a desk in a small office. When he was invited in to be interviewed, he had a shock. It was a very large room, with a long conference table. Around the table there were at least ten people! He sat at one end of the table and for two hours they asked him, in turn, the most difficult questions that he had ever been asked to answer in his life. He came out of the interview exhausted, and sure that he had failed to get the sole Leverhulme Scholarship that would be awarded for the next academic year.

In this he was quite right, and a letter arrived for him the following week. He had failed to get the Scholarship, but he was instead offered a place at the College, provided that he could pass Economics at Grade B in the General Certificate of Education, Advanced Level examinations. For the next six months he took a correspondence course to get this extra qualification and, of course, given his previous study of the subject, obtained this requirement easily.

The only problem was his mother; how could he leave her on her own and go up to London? As a Mature Student he would get a full grant for his university fees and his accommodation. He could send her some money, but they had grown to rely on his bank salary to help both of them live. "I want you to take up this great opportunity, dear," she had said to him. But Edwards knew that she would be lonely without him. His father had sent him a new watch, some twelve months before, for his twenty-first birthday, and they were now in touch with him again by letter. He was now camped out, sleeping on somebody's sofa who he had met down in a West Country city!

One day, his mother announced that she had received a letter from his father, and that he was coming to see them. When he arrived he stayed in a nearby, cheap bed and breakfast hotel. He came to see them several times, but Edwards still felt that he could never speak warmly again to his father, as he could never forgive him for what he had done in the past to ruin all their lives. After his father had left, his mother told him bluntly: "I will let you settle in at University first, but then I have agreed to re-join your father. We have decided that we will live in the same seaside resort in Devon, where some of our old friends have now retired to live."

Edwards was nonplus about this news. "Are you really sure, Mother?" he asked her.

"Yes, dear," replied his mother. "Despite all that he has done, I still love him. We will manage somehow. I still have some money saved that your grandfather left me when he died a few years ago, and I still have my little income from the bank's charity fund that my father arranged for me to get. Soon, both your father and I will qualify for some kind of reduced State Pension. Your father has also promised to find some proper part-time job to do, once we are firmly settled there."

Over the next few weeks, they talked about his father. For the first time, his mother told him something of his father's life before they had met and their early life together. When she came to talk about their wedding, she told him as well about their honeymoon in the South of France and how, one day, they had both received a terrible shock when a letter had arrived for her from her own mother. "She said that she was leaving my father and going to live with another man," she told Edwards. "What was so hurtful was that she said that I should never try and find her! Your own father reacted very badly. He became moody, despite him trying to comfort me. He thought that he was marrying into a stable family and one of the best families in the area. His own parents had both died, before we had met, and I think that he was looking forward to being part of my family. Instead of which, it immediately all fell apart, in a terrible mess!"

It was only slowly, and as he got older and more mature, that Edwards began to understand how his father had perhaps been affected by this event, so early in his marriage, and how it had probably "sowed the seeds" for the later disaster that his addiction to gambling had brought about. His father had been, perhaps, too weak. But, then, all human beings are frail in one way or another. But Edwards did learn from what had happened, during his younger life.

He also learned that love can never be finally denied, but we can never know the long-standing results of our love, and the results of the decisions that we take about our own lives, every day, on the lives of others. The Law of Unintended Consequences is very strong and it can, over time, affect those that we love, without our ever realising why, or what, has happened. But as human beings, without love, we have not lived. All we can do is to be always honest with each other, and trust each other until, perhaps sometimes, we suddenly realise that in some way, our trust has been irretrievably betrayed. Life can only really be understood by looking backwards, but it can only be truly lived, by looking forwards, in hope and optimism.

THE CAUSE

"A spectre is haunting Europe – the spectre of communism." – the first sentence of the *Manifesto of the Communist Party* by Karl Marx and Friedrich Engels.

1

For the first time in his life, Edwards was really frightened! He was much taller than Edwards and was carrying a long, heavy, steel bar. He was also very angry as his plans to demolish the large gate that Edwards was bravely standing in front of, were being frustrated. It was 1968, and it had started off as a demonstration against the School authorities, mimicking some of the recent violent student demonstrations that had taken place in the United States, and in Paris and other European cities. Their route had led from Trafalgar Square, along The Strand, to the short, narrow street where the School buildings stood. But then the demonstrating students had decided to storm the main building, easily brushing aside the security guards who had tried to stop them.

They had then occupied the main Lecture Theatre on the ground floor. They now wanted to occupy some of the upper floors, but the gate at the bottom of the stairs, installed, along with others, by the School authorities who had expected trouble, stood in their way. Edwards, along with some of his fellow students, were just as determined to stop them. Their further education was beginning to be jeopardised by the continuing activities of these radical fellow students. Several countries in Europe had, in the last few days, been swept by a chain of protests against their respective governments. Most of these demonstrations had been led by university students, and Britain was proving not to be an exception.

The odd thing was that Edwards knew this man who was now threatening him. He was a leading member of the so-called "Socialist Society", the majority of the members of which, for some reason, really believed in the political philosophy propounded by Karl Marx or Leon Trotsky. They were apologists for the actions of the Soviet Union and, despite the fact that he had killed millions of his own countrymen and women, supported the past actions of the former Soviet dictator, Joseph Stalin.

When he had arrived at university, Edwards had joined both the student club supporting the Conservative Party, as well as, to add a little variety, the Socialist Society. He had attended a number of the meetings of the latter, and had got to know the leading members of this student society. Like the man who was now confronting him, these leading members, both men and women, came from a privileged background. Edwards had found them intellectually arrogant, prejudiced, and totally intolerant of those that dared to disagree with them. Most of them were very intelligent, came from the upper-middle class, and had attended expensive private schools. They had led a pampered existence, until they had left home.

But at university, they still had plenty of their parent's money to spend, and some choose to spend it on supporting radical political activity. They could really afford to be Socialists! Edwards could not understand how they had become so radicalised; unless it was that they felt that they had now to turn against their previous closeted existence? Did they really suffer from some kind of guilt complex about their previous lives, and their parent's wealth? Or were they merely determined to keep their family's natural leadership, in any situation that they found themselves in? From his own previous difficult experiences of life, Edwards knew that you had to have been denied many things, and to have experienced real hardship, to then really appreciate what was afterwards offered to you.

The atmosphere in the School, which was a college of London University, was febrile and somewhat paranoid. Some students believed that they had identified other students who were agents working for the British MI5, whose real name was the Security Service. Some American graduate students were believed to be working for their Central Intelligence Agency, and even some other students were rumoured to be working for the Russian intelligence agency the K.G.B.!

Edwards had even been approached by his own Personal Tutor, a suave academic who, in the past, had acted as an adviser to government. At one of his private tutorials, this man had indicated to Edwards that, maybe, he should give him some information on his more radical fellow students, who were obviously thinking the wrong way. Edwards had declined, mainly because he thought it was morally wrong to inform on his fellow students, but also because he thought that at this stage in his life, he was not yet really temperamentally suited to be a spy!

"Move out of my way or I will smash you down too," shouted the student carrying the long steel bar, at Edwards.

Edwards, who did not feel at all confident, tried to fix him in the eye. "I don't think that you will do that, Mike," he retorted. Mike snorted in derision at him.

Just then, two more students, who thought in a similar way to Edwards, joined him. Together, despite the threat of the long steel bar, they slowly but firmly pushed Mike back from the gate that he wanted to destroy.

The rest of the radical students were now celebrating their occupation of the School and were attending a series of heated speeches by their leaders, in the main Lecture Theatre. They had all brought the means to camp out overnight in the college, but Edwards and his colleagues, who were certainly in the minority, had not. As the evening wore on, they began to drift away. Edwards, at last, decided to walk back to his Hall of Residence. He now sensed a feeling of resentment, or even hate against him, from some of the radical students who knew him and who were now patrolling the corridors of the School. He had now been recognised as an enemy; after attending the meetings of the Socialist Society for about nine months, he had been identified as a "Capitalist Spy", and had been forced out of the Society.

These privileged, radical leaders, found no difficulty in finding followers. Usually, they were students from poorer backgrounds or those who, perhaps, were not so intelligent as their leaders. They had no experience of the real world and were so easily led into supporting the Radical Cause by the idealism, and the "black and white" philosophy that their leaders put forward.

There were undoubtedly some good speakers among the student leaders. They had been taught how to speak publically and how to argue during their expensive, private education. The others easily became their "foot soldiers," just used to swell the number of demonstrators and to carry out the tasks that their leaders allocated to them. You were classed by these leaders either as a "True Believer" in Communism, or as a "Lackey of the Capitalist System." If you tried to make a stand against what these radicals were doing or believed in, then you were accused simply of being a "Fascist," or an "Enemy of the Downtrodden Masses!"

Such was the unfortunate prevailing political atmosphere in the School: sensible and polite debate between the two sides was impossible. You were either "one of us," or "against us." Unfortunately, Edwards had the disadvantage of already having had six years of experience in the real world and, after a while, the world of student politics began to bore him. All he wanted to do was to carry on with his studies, and qualify with a good degree in Economics at the end of his three years at university.

2

When Edwards had left Wales and come up to London in the early autumn of 1967, he had decided to book himself into a

THE CAUSE

Hall of Residence within easy walking distance of his college, for his first year of university. This would enable him to "find his feet" for his first time in the big city. He was allocated to a Hall that consisted of a number of Regency houses, that had been joined together, and which were located in the part of London known as Bloomsbury. Around it, were a number of typical London squares, filled with trees, flower beds, and grassy areas. Some were private squares, available to residents only, but others were open to the public. As well as park benches, in the spring and summer, deck chairs were available to rent for the hour or the day. On a warm summer day, it was just delightful to sit and read or study in one of these squares.

This area of Bloomsbury contained Senate House, which was the headquarters of the University of London, the British Museum, and many Regency buildings from the early 19th century. It was famous for the historic Bloomsbury Group, a set of associated writers, intellectuals, and artists who had lived there in the early 20th century. These included the economist John Maynard Keynes, on whose work most of modern Economics was based. After the end of the First World War, Keynes had argued strongly against the "Reparations", that the defeated Germany was forced to pay, and which became one of the major reasons for the Second World War. Keynes was also credited with the economic policies that were finally brought into place, to try and increase employment and reduce poverty after the Great Crash of 1929, which had then led to the Great Depression of the 1930s.

Because he had already worked for six years in a bank, Edwards was viewed as a Mature Student. He received a full grant for his university fees and his living expenses. He was naturally frugal but, nevertheless, managed to eke out a reasonably enjoyable existence. The disadvantage was that, in his first year, he had to share a room with three other students. They were, of course, all younger than him, and sometimes looked to him for advice, which he gladly gave. He was fortunate and was elected onto the Student Committee, which helped to run the Hall. This meant that he was allowed to stay on there for the following two academic years, so that he did not have to find rented accommodation with other students. In his second year, he only had to share with one other student and in the third and final year, he was finally given his own single room.

He loved the social life in this large, rambling residence: the idea of a shared house or flat with a small number of other students, did not appeal to him. Being older, he was more at home with the post-graduate students who also lived in the Hall. He found that, as many were studying for a further Master's, or even Doctor's degrees, his intellectual ability and discourse had to rise markedly, in order to fit in with them and their conversation. They were a mixed bunch; as well as the British there were Germans, Swedes, Indians, and of course, Americans. They met regularly together, to share a meal, or just some bottles of wine.

Among them was a German girl whose main claim to fame was that she had read and largely memorised both volumes of "Das Kapital" by Karl Marx. This book had been originally published in German in 1867. On several evenings there had been very emotional arguments between her and an American male graduate student, as to what a particular paragraph, or even a particular sentence, said, how it should be understood, or how it should be translated into English. These usually ended when one of them went to find and bring back their copy of "Das Kapital". They were both avowed Marxists but, somehow, inevitably, she was always right!

Edwards was at first amused by their evangelical disputes to prove the other one wrong, but then he realised how passionately they both held their beliefs, and how, having such attitudes, could so easily lead to hate, and then to the persecution of, people who just did not agree with your own views.

Edwards had to conclude that Marxism was just like any other form of religion. Only the less intelligent actually believed in it. There was a middle group of believers who went along with it, particularly in the then Communist countries, for the better lifestyle that it brought them. But the most intelligent adopted it for their own ends, as they saw it as a way that could bring them into power. Marxism seemed to be based upon sowing hate and division in society, in the hope that this would lead to a violent revolution, which would then bring the cleverer Marxist leaders to power.

Then there was a graduate Swedish student, she was tall and blonde with an excellent figure. She was not interested in politics, only in having a good time. While the male members of the group lusted after her, she would have none of them. Instead, she began an affair with the resident University Tutor who ran the Hall from a large flat at one end of the building, where he lived with his wife and children. Finally, when she had finished her course, he left his wife and children in London, and they eloped together to Canada, where he had found a new university post in one of the great rolling Prairie Provinces. Just a few years later, she was killed in his car, in a horrific car crash, with a fire engine on its way to a blaze!

Edwards enjoyed the cultural activity of this group. One of them had a subscription to the Royal Opera House in Covent Garden and could purchase as many tickets as he wanted. The Opera House was in easy walking distance of the Hall, and members of the group regularly attended. As well as opera, Edwards found that he enjoyed performances by the Royal Ballet. Several times they were very lucky and obtained tickets for a performance by the then leading ballet dancers in the world, Margot Fonteyn, and the Russian defector, Rudolf Nureyev. Edwards was stunned by the sheer energy and skill of their performances, as was the rest of the packed audience. After one of their performances, Edwards noted that the entire audience was still on their feet applauding them, over one hour after the performance had ended! In all, this famous couple took a total of twenty-four "curtain calls" that evening, and the memory of their magnificent performances remained with Edwards for years after they had happened.

3

By now Edwards had his own "cause" to follow; after the struggle to finish his school education, and his years of work, study, and deprivation, he was determined to become a more rounded individual. The intensity of his social life was matched by his studies. As well as the books that he thought that he had to read for his economics degree course, he was determined to read more widely. In particular, philosophy and comparative religion interested him, but he also read works on history and psychology, and the lives of the great artists and composers.

He visited the British Museum, and he could be seen, also, in the many other museums and art galleries that London had to offer.

Edwards' interest in music began to blossom. He bought himself a good record player and began to collect both classical and more modern music, all on 33 rpm, vinyl records. In his third year, with a small room to himself, he could play what and when he liked. That was usually Beethoven, Mozart, or Wagner, played as loudly as possible, before his neighbours started to complain! His other loves were the songs of Nina Simone and Simon and Garfunkel. The latter music inspired his wish to visit America.

At the end of his last university year, before he started to work again, this was achieved. He took part in a Student Exchange scheme; a Canadian student came to Britain, and Edwards flew to Winnipeg in Manitoba, where he was to work for three months for a large Canadian insurance company. He enjoyed the friendly openness of the Canadians, and the dry summer heat of the Prairie Provinces. He found himself a spare bedroom, within an easy walk of his work, in the high-rise apartment of a caring, elderly lady, who provided him with his meals. From his window, he often watched the incredible summer lightning storms that crossed the prairies. No rain, no thunder, merely a huge natural fireworks display!

At the end of the three months, he had earned enough money to finance his further travels. He purchased a "99 Dollar" Greyhound Bus ticket; it was in fact a book of tickets, valid for one month, and, once you had used up all the vouchers in the book, with numerous Greyhound bus journeys, you could claim another book of tickets. From Winnipeg, he took the Trans-Canadian Highway first to Toronto, and then on to Montreal, and Quebec City. He included a visit, by Greyhound, to the Niagara Falls, and to the battlefield of the Plains of Abraham, where Wolfe had defeated the French Army and had claimed Canada for Britain. Heading south, he crossed the United States border and, after travelling through the glorious state of Vermont, he arrived in Boston.

Previously he had stayed with friends, introduced by his work colleagues back in Winnipeg, but now he had nowhere to stay. He wandered through the Boston University precinct, and got talking to some of the students. They took him to a Hall of Residence, which found him a room. From there he explored the sights of Boston, and spent one day in the suburb of Cambridge, including a walk around the Harvard University campus and a visit to the Harvard Art Museum. On the Greyhound, he took a day's trip to the small resort of Hyannis Port where the Kennedy family had their summer residence. At the end of his stay in Boston, he went to pay for his room. The Hall's Treasurer looked at him; "You are from the Old Country," he said. "You do not need to pay us anything."

Another Greyhound bus took Edwards south to New Haven in Connecticut, the home of Yale University. There he stayed with a graduate student he had met at university, who had now returned to Yale to continue their studies. After that he travelled further south to New York, where he had booked himself, for a week, into the dubious charms of the Times Square Motor Hotel, located on the corner of 43rd Street and 8th Avenue. The building was in a state of disrepair and seemed to be peopled by deprived and depraved guests! At night, there were the shouts and screams of drug addicts, and the toilets and washing areas were run-down and dirty. Edwards locked his door carefully, and tried to avoid any contact with the other hotel guests! Instead, he tried to spend as little time as possible in his hotel, and to enjoy New York as best as he could.

It was very hot and sultry. One day, he took the cheapest sightseeing tour available: a return trip on the Staten Island Ferry. Then he took another ferry to the Statue of Liberty from Battery Park, at the southern tip of Manhattan. In those days, you could climb up the inside of the Statue and Edwards was determined to do that. This day was marked out as a "95/95" day: 95 degrees Fahrenheit and 95 per cent humidity! Inside the Statue it was like an oven, and when he reached the ground again, he was soaked in perspiration. But he also wanted to see the cultural side of New York, visiting the Guggenheim Museum, the Museum of Modern Art, and the Metropolitan Museum of Art. He also found the time to visit the Frick Collection, and the American Museum of Natural History.

His week in New York flew by. He had found good, and safe, places to eat around the area of his hotel. He was lucky, his possessions were not stolen. Although he kept away from his hotel as much as he could, he had to return fearfully, to sleep there every night. At the end of the week, he took another Greyhound Bus to Washington. He was due to stay with the parents of his student friend now at Yale University but, unfortunately, he had arrived at the Bus Terminal very late in the evening. He found a telephone booth, in the Bus Station, and called them.

"Where are you?" they asked, so he told them. "Don't move," came the immediate reply. "Whatever you do, stay in the Terminal, and we will come to collect you as soon as we can get there!"

Edwards could not understand their concerns, until he looked around properly. The Bus Terminal was filled with dubious-looking people of every description! In the middle of the crowded Bus Terminal stood a very large, black policeman. He had one hand on his holstered gun, and from the other hand he was twirling a long, heavy baton. Edwards went to stand next to him, until he was finally collected by the father of his friend. His wife did not stop their car, but drove it around the Bus Terminal until she saw them waiting outside for her!

After his rescue, he enjoyed his time with the civilised parents of his friend. They lived in a suburb on the Washington Beltway, close to Interstate 495, which encircled Washington. It was an easy journey for him to take a local bus into the city every morning. Again he visited the usual tourist sites, but also the museums and art galleries, including those within the vast Smithsonian Institute. One day, he took an extra bus trip to visit Mount Vernon, on the bank of the Potomac River, the house and plantation of George Washington, the first President of the United States. Behind the main house were the small buildings, where Washington kept his black slaves.

He was suitably grateful to his kind hosts; everywhere he had gone in North America, as a representative of the "Old Country", he had been treated well and offered so much hospitality. On the road again, he visited Richmond for the day. As the old Confederate capital in the Civil War, it interested him, and he visited several of the institutes in its "Museum District." He was determined to make his final visit: another overnight

Greyhound bus from Richmond took him to Jacksonville in Florida, and then on another Greyhound down south to the Cape Kennedy Space Centre in Central Florida. Edwards had been fascinated with the arrival of men on the Moon, and he wanted to see the base from which they had departed. The great rockets on display thrilled him, and the building in which they had been assembled and stored was so vast, that clouds could form in its upper storeys.

From Cape Kennedy, he returned by Greyhound bus to New York, and then flew home to restart his banking career at a leading merchant bank in the financial district of the City of London. For the first time, after his years of deprivation, he felt that he had been successful in his "Cause", to become a more rounded, cultivated, and well-travelled individual! Three years of living in the centre of radical student politics had not deterred him, and the cultural pleasures of London were still a great attraction. His "Grand Tour" of the United States had been much more than an education in itself.

4

Despite Edwards's efforts to "defend the gates," the next day they were demolished by the radical students. They continued to occupy the School, but gradually, their number diminished as their less committed followers drifted away. But the keepers of law and order had not given up and one evening, when most of the occupying students were in the bar, the Metropolitan Police, in great numbers, entered the School at the invitation of the College Authorities. They then cleared out the students, taking the names of the suspected leaders of the occupation. These leaders were then excluded by the School Authorities, from entering the premises in future. The police then locked all the entrances and occupied the School, for the next several months. Lectures had to be transferred to other University buildings in Central London, and the School was only reopened after the College Authorities had brought in some new rules on discipline, and the conduct of the students.

Edwards, and the majority of students who thought like him, were relieved to be able to get on at last with their studies, unmolested by this radicalised and selfish minority element of the student body. In later life he would always amusingly say, when asked about his college years, that "When he had entered University, his political beliefs were somewhere to the liberal end of the Conservative Party. But, when he had left University, he was politically somewhere to the right of Genghis Khan!"

But Edwards never forgot what he had learnt about radicalisation and continued to hate the extreme and uncompromising positions taken up by radicals, be they political, or religious in nature. The great political philosopher Michael Oakeshott, who had taught at the School, believed that the political spectrum was not a straight line between "Left or Right" but was, in fact, a circle with the liberal and democratic beliefs at its centre, and the more extreme political creeds, on its diameter. That way, the beliefs of Communism and Fascism were, in fact, very close to each other. But Edwards remained a student of history, and read widely about the real political revolutions that, in the past, had actually taken place.

Although there had always been some form of dissent in society, which he believed was healthy, a true Revolution only took place when the conditions of life for the ordinary people, had been much reduced by outside circumstances. Only then could the minority of the political radicals, in any society, gain the support of the majority of the people. Most people were conservative in their outlook, and were content to continue with their ordinary, daily lives, as long as their living standards were not seriously compromised. It took a great reduction in their material circumstances to motivate them to take any action against the status quo.

The examples that Edwards always had in mind were the French Revolution, which began in 1789, and the Russian Revolution of 1917. In both cases, the ordinary people had faced a rapid decline in their standard of living. In the first case, with heavily increased taxation to meet the costs of the French King supporting the American colonists against the British. In the second case, it was the virtual defeat and economic collapse, as a result of Russian participation in the First World War, that had resulted in the Marxists eventually taking charge. That terrible war, with its vast loss of life, had also brought about the revolutionary collapse of the defeated German, Austro-Hungarian, and Ottoman Empires.

A true Revolution is always steeped in blood, and results in chaos. It is then often taken over by a ruthless strongman, to bring back order. To Edwards, the names of Napoleon Bonaparte, Vladimir Ilyich Ulyanov, better known as Lenin, Adolf Hitler and, more benignly, Mustafa Kemal Ataturk, came to mind. The efforts of the student revolutionaries of his college days, were, fortunately, doomed to failure. At that time, Britain had enjoyed a period of many years of growth, and a continuing increase in the standard of living of the ordinary people. These intellectual radicals could never, in these circumstances, inspire the true working classes to throw away the economic gains that they had so recently acquired. To quote the patrician, Conservative Prime Minister, Harold Macmillan, in 1957: "Most of our people have never had it so good!"

BY THE LAKES

"Switzerland is a country where few things begin, but many things end." – F. Scott Fitzgerald.

1

Edwards sat up in the large bed, and looked out of the picture window. He had left the curtains open the night before, so that he could enjoy the view of the sunset. It was 1974, and Edwards was still unmarried. He was working in the City of London for a well-known merchant bank. Outside the hotel window, there was the balcony of his hotel room. It was just wide enough to hold two chairs and a small table. It was a cloudless day and, below the balcony, the waters of the large lake perfectly reflected the blue sky, in the early-morning sunshine. Beyond the waters of the lake, as far as one could see, the sunlight was also glinting off the high, dramatic, snow-topped Swiss Alps. Besides Edwards, still asleep, lay his Swiss girlfriend; she was tall, blonde, and beautiful, with a very fine figure.

There had been only a few times, in his past life, that he had felt a lucky man. But now was one of them. They had arrived the previous evening, from the small town north of Zurich, where she lived with her parents. It was just past the normal tourist season so they had been easily given a superior room, when she had asked the Receptionist in her rather strange Schweizerdeutsch dialect, if they could be upgraded at the same price. She was immediately recognised as a local Swiss girl, and then everything became possible! Edwards understood only a little German, but the German spoken by some of the Swiss, was nothing like the Haute-Deutsch that he had been taught. Even the heavy, Bavarian German accent, was nothing like it, it was a language completely on its own.

But then Switzerland was a strange land, with four languages, and three different national groups. Edwards already knew Ticino, the Italian speaking part of Switzerland to the south. Some years before, when he had been working in the International Bond Market, he had been given Italy and Ticino as areas to travel to and market his firm's expertise. His regular visits had been to Milan and Lugano. Lugano was on the shores of the beautiful Lake Lugano, but Edwards was literally running around this Swiss city, from bank to bank, having meetings in each one. This meant that he had no time to take in the fine views of the lake, and the high snow-capped mountains surrounding it. But his travels to there had ended, and he was now working for a different company.

Then there was the French speaking part of the country, home to the city of Geneva. Some years before, he had travelled there and stayed with a family that he had been introduced to, by a friend back in London. The husband had taken him camping for a few nights in the mountains high above Geneva, with a wonderful view over Lake Geneva itself. After a reasonably comfortable night inside the tent, he had been woken up the following morning by a unique Swiss sound. Around them, in the high pasture, were gathered a herd of cows, and each cow had around its neck a large cowbell. So the first sound that he had heard that morning, was a musical crescendo of Swiss cow bells!

Back in the city, he had walked around the shore of the Lake of Geneva, to take in the view of the great Jet d'Eau water fountain, and to visit the Palace of Nations and the other United Nations buildings. The Palace of Nations had been built during the 1930's, to serve as a home for the ill-fated League of Nations organisation. This had been formed in an effort to keep the peace after the terrible experience of the first great global conflict of 1914-18. He had also visited some of the churches of Geneva, and the Reformation Wall which honoured in stone many of the individuals, events, and documents of the Protestant Reformation.

In the isolated south-eastern Swiss canton of Grisons, the Romansh language was also spoken, which was a form of

Latin strongly influenced by German. There were twenty-six Swiss cantons all together, which made up the member states of the Swiss Confederation. These had all been once separate, sovereign states, until they had been brought together in the Swiss Federal State in 1848. With this history, Switzerland was thus a very loose gathering of small, formerly independent nations, and any central political decisions had to be carefully balanced to take in the views of the individual cantons and its people.

The only thing that seemed to bring its people together was the sense that they were all Swiss in the end and that they had to defend themselves and their high standard of living, against any invader. Because of this diversity, the Swiss made very regular use of Referendums, either national, or at a more local level. Then the views of the people would be directly asked for, even on some small and seemingly unimportant matters.

After a good breakfast, Edwards drove them both along the lake to the city of Lucerne. This charming Medieval city was located on the banks of Lake Lucerne or, as it is known in German, the Vierwaldstattersee. In English, this is usually translated as: "The Lake of the Four Cantons", since four separate Swiss cantons border on to the lake. He parked his car and then, just like any other tourists, they indulged in some sightseeing. They first walked along the famous Kapellbrücke over the lake; originally built in 1333, it was the oldest covered bridge in Europe. Inside the bridge were a series of seventeenth century paintings depicting events from the long history of Lucerne. His girlfriend had never visited Lucerne before, and she had been rather excited that they were going there.

Edwards was sometimes amused by the Swiss as they were inherently very conservative, and rarely left the area where they had been born, except to go to foreign countries. When he had once told his girlfriend and her parents that he was going on, from them, to visit his friends in Geneva, they had treated this news as if he was now travelling to a distant, foreign, and rather dangerous country!

From the Kapellbrücke, they found their way to the Church of St. Leodegar, named after the city's Patron Saint, and built on a small hill above the lake front. Dating back to the eight century, it had been rebuilt in late Renaissance style in 1633. By now, it was nearing the time for lunch, and they found a restaurant in the Old Town, housed within a half-timbered building with an obviously old, but heavily retouched, painted front. His girlfriend wanted to spend the afternoon "window-shopping" in the Old Town and, although it bored him, Edwards felt that he just had to comply. By now, he had realised, that if you really wanted a woman, you had to comply with her wishes, however strange these might seem to be!

Back in their hotel, they decided that, rather than go out to get dinner, they would take a chance on the hotel dining-room. It was small, but not crowded, and indeed there was only one other couple having dinner there. They appeared to be middle-aged locals, and seemed to be fascinated by the conversation between Edwards and his partner. Having ordered the dinner in her local Swiss dialect, she turned to Edwards and begun to speak to him in English. His girlfriend spoke excellent English; she had visited England many times, and had previously worked, for a while, as a low-paid helper in a Children's Home in a London suburb.

Edwards rarely used her German Christian name, as he did not like it. Instead, he sometimes used a shortened form of it, but then decided to give her his own nickname of "Muffy". As they spoke together, they held hands. The local Swiss couple in the dining room had looked at them, at first, suspiciously, but now they looked at them disapprovingly. Why was a local Swiss girl in an intimate conversation with a man who was obviously an Englishman? After their meal, they returned to their room. Again Edwards opened the curtains so that, sitting up in their bed, they could view another magnificent sunset over the lake and the snow-covered mountains behind.

When the darkness finally came, they began to cuddle together and then to kiss. Muffy was not inexperienced in sexual matters, and she was not shy in coming forward. After a few minutes, she had straddled Edwards, and was very enthusiastically preparing to accommodate him. Then it had happened! A large tourist boat, only partly full, complete with many coloured, flashing lights and a loud brass band, playing Swiss folk tunes, arrived outside their window. Rather than just passing by, it seemed to stop and anchor itself there, while the brass band played on.

Muffy was reduced to giggles; "Sorry, I can't do this now," she laughed, sliding off him. "They will see my bottom going up and down under the duvet!" A very frustrated Edwards tried to reassure her that the tourists outside could not possibly see into their room. But it was no good, and it was not until after the boat had, at last, left, that they were able to resume their night-time activities.

2

Edwards had only learnt to drive in the year following his time at university. After his final university results, he had gone to work in Canada for the summer and had then toured the Eastern Seaboard of Canada and the United States, using the Greyhound bus network. When he returned to London, he had joined a prestigious merchant bank in the City of London. He had found himself a bed-sitting room to live in, located just off the Kings Road in Chelsea. The London of the early 1970's was no longer the "Swinging London" of the 1960's, the end of which era, Edwards had just managed to experience. But Chelsea was still fashionable, with its cafés and smart boutiques. Edwards liked to sit in a café and watch the pretty, well-dressed girls, known as the "Sloane Rangers", as they paraded, ostentatiously, along the Kings Road.

He took some driving lessons, but failed at his first attempt to pass the Driving Test. He changed his Driving Instructor and took some more lessons; one day his Driving Instructor had terrified him by taking him to practice his driving around Marble Arch, along Park Lane and then around the large, crowded roundabout at its end. "If you can drive along here, you can drive anywhere," his Driving Instructor had said. It had worked! Edwards had passed his Driving Test at his second attempt.

Then he had bought his first car: a dark blue classically styled Citroen DS with its unique suspension that he thought had once saved his life! He used to drive regularly up from London to Aberdeen, to visit a close friend from his university days. He had since moved to the "Granite City" and had been lecturing at Aberdeen University for several years. On one dark night,

Edwards had been overtaking a long, heavy lorry, driving much too fast on the two-lane carriageway of the then A74 road, between the Scottish border and Glasgow. He had come off the road on to a grass verge, and the Citroen had not overturned, but had spun around three or four times.

The lorry driver had stopped his vehicle and had come to see if Edwards was alright. "I thought that you had had it!" he had said.

"No, I am fine, thank you," said Edwards. He restarted his engine, which had stalled, and drove back on to the road, and then away, at full speed.

When you are young, you tend to think of yourself as immortal; Edwards and his friend in Aberdeen took to amateur rally driving, through the narrow, twisting roads and small villages of Royal Deeside, just west of Aberdeen. They set Time Trials against each other to see who could drive the fastest between two points. In winter, your main danger was black ice. Edwards grew used to looking for the tell-tail, diamond-like glint from the road surface, on the freezing days of deep winter. Going up to Scotland he used the M6 motorway, keeping his speed as high as he possibly could. On one night-time return journey from Aberdeen to London, he managed the 550 miles trip, which included long stretches of ordinary roads as well, in just under eight hours. On the long motorway sections of the journey, he had held his speedometer needle between 100 and 120 miles an hour all the way.

For Edwards, the German autobahn network provided fast, relaxed driving on his way to Switzerland. There were no speed limits on much of the German motorways at that time. But you had to be careful, sometimes the road would suddenly narrow from three lanes in one direction, down to two lanes. Then you hit the notorious "Caterpillars" where, in the two-lane sections, slower car drivers moved out to the fast lane, to overtake even slower moving heavy vehicles.

It was once in one of those two lane sections, that a large, distinctly- coloured Mercedes had suddenly appeared behind him. It flashed its headlights and sounded its horn. Edwards respectfully withdrew to the slow lane, and the Mercedes roared past him at a speed, Edwards estimated, of 130 miles an hour! Beginning to feel tired, he decided to pull in at the next Service Station, and there was the distinctive Mercedes with its German number plate. He parked opposite it, and rested his head back for a short sleep. But then the Mercedes driver appeared, and Edwards watched them return to their vehicle. The driver was a little old lady of at least eighty years old, walking slowly on two crutches! She propelled herself into the driving seat, rested her two crutches beside her, closed the door, and left the car park at a speed of at least 60 miles an hour!

His route to Zurich passed through Dover, Ostend, and the Belgium motorway system. The latter by-passed Brussels, and was always lit brightly at night. Then he drove east to Cologne and down Germany to the Swiss border, just north of Zurich. He found that this journey was becoming too regular a habit, but only once did he take the plane and the train. This time he decided to combine his visit to Zurich, with visits first to Munich and then to Vienna. He flew to Munich, took the train on to Vienna, then a night train to Zurich, before flying back to London.

In Munich, he stayed with some friends of his friend in Aberdeen. They lived in Schwabing, which was then considered to be the avant-garde suburb of Munich, with its accumulation of bars, night clubs, and restaurants. He walked in the Englischer Garten, took in some of the other sights, and one evening attended a performance of the Bavarian State Opera.

But it was the second half of September, and he had the opportunity of seeing Bavarian culture at first hand. One evening he was taken by his friends to visit the Oktoberfest! Held in the fairground of Theresienwiese, it consisted of a number of very large tents or marquees. Each tent had numerous tables and benches inside them, and each belonged to a different Munich brewery. In the centre of each tent was a raised dais, on which a brass band blasted out Bavarian folk tunes and drinking songs. Large portions of fried chicken in a basket were served with pommes frites, accompanied by plenty of heavy, litre stein glasses of beer. All the beer had been brewed especially for this annual festival. Everybody in the tent joined in to sing the drinking songs, very loudly, and a good time was had by all!

In Vienna, he unashamedly took to the main tourist routes, including a visit to the Schönbrunn Palace, and the Spanish Riding School. For two evenings, during his stay, he visited the Vienna State Opera for magnificent Mozart opera performances. On the evening of his departure, he was due to leave on the "Wiener Walzer" night train, to Zurich. While he was sitting, waiting for his train at the Vienna Hauptbahnhof, he noticed a young man, in full evening dress, waiting on the opposite platform. A local train pulled into this platform, and what happened next, was an example of true Austrian manners.

A much older couple descended from the newly arrived local train, also dressed immaculately in evening clothes. The younger man strode forward to meet them. He stopped in front of the older man, clicked his heels and bowed in salute. "Guten

Abend, Herr, Professor, Doctor, Doctor," he said in a loud voice, clicked his heels again, and took the older man's extended hand. Turning to the lady, he again clicked his heels, bowed, and recited "Guten Abend, Frau, Professor, Doctor, Doctor," He clicked his heals again, took the lady's proffered gloved hand, bowed his head even lower, and kissed her hand. "Only in Vienna, would I witness such a scene," thought Edwards, to himself. "Here, they still follow the formal social graces of the former Austro-Hungarian Empire." He had learnt that not only had the Professor been awarded double Doctorate degrees, but also that any higher-class Austrian wife, would always take on the full and proper titles of her husband in any such social situation.

3

The "Wiener Walzer" proved to be just that; Edwards had to cling on to his narrow bunk as the train seemed to be taking many, major bends in the track, at speed. He realised that there was probably spectacular mountain scenery outside, and promised himself to take this journey again, in daylight, if he ever had the chance. He arrived at Zurich, just after dawn, and then took the local train to the small town where Muffy lived with her parents. Her parents had now accepted his regular visits: they had a three-bedroom apartment in a well-maintained block of flats. He was always given Muffy's brother's bedroom. Her brother, fortunately, always seemed to be away whenever he visited, working in another part of Switzerland.

After he had recovered from his overnight journey, they went out together to get some lunch in the small town. Dinner was held at home with her parents who, although they could speak very little English, always welcomed him warmly and tried to make themselves understood to him. He was tired, so he retired to bed early. At about one o'clock his bedroom door opened silently, and then closed again. Muffy had come from her bedroom, along the corridor; she took off her nightdress and snuggled into the rather hard, single bed, with Edwards.

The following morning, they took the local train into Zurich together, as Muffy had to work that day. Being a Swiss train, it left the local station at precisely the right second on the station clock, as shown on the timetable. She worked in the office of a Swiss Bank; Edwards had been introduced to her by a German University friend who now worked for the London branch of the same bank. Muffy had come over for a six-month secondment to the London branch, and one weekend she had been invited to lunch by Edwards's friend and his wife, who lived in an eastern suburb of London. Edwards had been their other guest.

After lunch, they had driven to a fair on the seafront of Southend-on-Sea and competed together, as two couples, on the dodgem cars. Afterwards, Edwards had driven Muffy to a railway station, to catch the train back to the small flat that her bank had rented for her. He kissed her goodnight, and given her enthusiastic reaction, decided instead to drive her all the way back to her flat! After that, they met as regularly as they could. But then, too quickly, Muffy's stay in London had come to an end, and she had to return back home to Switzerland.

She now talked to Edwards openly about her work at the bank. She was part of a small team that dealt with the numbered accounts. These accounts did not bear a name, but only a number. They were held by people from abroad who, for one reason or another, wanted to keep their money abroad, free of tax, and away from the prying eyes of their own government. With the established Swiss Banking Secrecy laws, their bank account number and their real identity was never brought together. There was one list that contained this vital information, and it was kept locked away. Only a small elite team of trusted bank officers could access it.

Although she was still fairly junior, Muffy had access to it. Her main task was to help in sending secret, coded messages to these customers. Each numbered account customer had been given a code book containing a series of phrases, which served as secret messages, and a copy of this was kept in the bank. These messages were most usually sent by a postcard; a stock of postcards was kept in the bank, showing typical tourist scenes in Switzerland, for this purpose. Muffy used to select a postcard, write the agreed secret message on it, and then sign it with the name agreed with the customer. She then added the customer's name and address on it, from the secret list, and then posted it. If she wrote "The Matterhorn looked really beautiful today," for example, when the bank customer received the postcard, they would consult their code book that they had been previously given, and would then understand this phrase to mean: "Your ten-million-dollar deposit has been safely received!"

Left to himself, Edwards walked around a little of Lake Zurich on which the city lay, visiting the Grossmünster, which dated back to the twelfth century. It was one of the four major Protestant churches in the city and the burial place of Felix and Regula, the Patron Saints of Zurich. He gazed at the statue of the great Protestant Reformer Huldrych Zwingli outside the ancient Wasserkirche church, and in the afternoon, he visited the Kunsthaus.

Edwards had already visited a number of major art galleries in other cities but, immediately, he was struck by the depth and numbers of the pictures on show here, particularly from the French Impressionist Period which he loved. By each picture was a small bronze plaque giving its name, the artist, and the year that it had been painted. In most cases, were added the words "From a Private Collection." Edwards quickly realised that these were pictures that were safely stored in Zurich, by their very rich owners, in order to hide away their wealth. Rather than just keep them in a bank vault, the owners had rightly agreed to exhibit them at the local Art Gallery, so that others could enjoy them. No doubt, the Gallery paid for their insurance, and they may have even paid a small fee to their owners from the extra entry fees to the gallery, generated by such wonderful pictures being there to be seen.

He met Muffy at the Zurich Hauptbahnhof, and they made their way together back to her parent's flat. After dinner with her parents, they all sat watching television. It was a boring program in a language that Edwards really did not understand. He went to his bedroom to do some things, and Muffy soon joined him.

"Do you know what you are sleeping on?" she suddenly asked.

"No," replied Edwards, a little bemused.

She moved his bedclothes aside and then the mattress; underneath was a large, hinged lid that she then opened. Edwards reeled back; inside was a moderately-sized arsenal! He could clearly see several automatic pistols, a high-powered semi-automatic rifle, a Sniper's rifle with a telescopic sight, a rocket-propelled grenade launcher complete with a grenade ready to fire, boxes of ammunition of various types, a box of rocket-propelled grenades, and a box of what looked like hand grenades. He quickly calculated that there were enough explosives stored there to destroy the whole block of flats!

"These are my brother's," she explained. "He is in the Swiss Army, and like all our other soldiers, he keeps his weapons at home." She explained that every fit, young Swiss male, was conscripted, on a part-time basis, into the Swiss Army, and that they all kept their weapons at home, ready to resist any invasion. Edwards remembered that every weekend that he had stayed in Switzerland, there was always the continuous sound of gunfire from the nearby forests, as every local male indulged in intensive target practice.

After that, Edwards became a little less certain about using this bed for Muffy's night time visits, although it did not seem to worry her at all. Anticipating her visits, when he thought that everybody else was asleep, he instead used to get up and creep quietly to her room, along the corridor, where he always received a very warm welcome. Unfortunately, it was next to her parent's room, which meant that now a certain level of discrete silence had to be maintained.

4

The next time that he travelled to Switzerland was in the spring of the following year. He took his car again, on his regular route of Dover, Ostend, through Belgium to Cologne, then south through Germany to the Swiss border. On this visit, he wanted to take Muffy to somewhere he used to visit before, Lugano, and then on to another lake that he had heard about: Lake Maggiore, which is half in Switzerland and half in Italy. Its climate is mild all the year round, helping Mediterranean flowers and vegetation to flourish. There are a number of lovely gardens that have been planted on its banks, or on islands in the middle of the lake, over the last hundreds of years. It is considered to be one of the most beautiful lakes in the world, and is surrounded by the peaks of the Southern Alps.

After two days staying with Muffy's parents, he drove them both from Zurich to Lugano, through spectacular mountain scenery. They crossed many bridges, over deep ravines, and drove through many tunnels, under the high mountains. As they crossed over one bridge, Muffy pointed out to him a large steel box, with a stout lock on it. The box was on a metal post in the middle of the bridge.

"Do you know what that is?" she asked. Edwards professed ignorance. "On nearly every bridge in Switzerland, and in every tunnel, there is one of those," Muffy informed him. "The key to each box is usually kept by an Old-Age Pensioner, who lives in the nearest village, and who has done military service. In the event of an invasion, they go to the box and open it. Inside are explosives and fuses. Their job is to lay the explosives, as they have been taught, light the fuse, and blow up the bridge or the tunnel."

Edwards could not help but to be impressed by Swiss efficiency, and their determination to defend their country. It gave him part of the answer to the question of why, through many European wars, Switzerland had never been invaded? It was just too difficult to do so! The other part of the answer was, of course, that the elites of the warring nations had to always have somewhere safe, stable and independent to keep their money and their valuables. After that, Edwards looked for the locked, steel box, as he drove over every bridge, and through every tunnel in Switzerland. It was always there!

After nearly a day of travelling, they arrived at their hotel in Lugano. Edwards had booked it only for three nights, just enough time to see a few things in the city which he had never had time to see before, during his previous visits. The next day, they walked along the promenade on the shore of Lake Lugano, gazing up at the wooded mountain slopes surrounding the lake. They took a paddle steamer, for a panoramic cruise on the lake, so that they could look back at the city; many of its buildings were built in the Italian classical style. Back on shore, they visited several of the Renaissance churches and then found themselves in the city's main square of the Piazza Riforma.

From there, Edwards could spot some of the banks that he used to visit. He told Muffy about his former visits, and how he used to run from bank to bank to make sure he was not late for his next meeting. As he ran, he used to talk into a Dictaphone to record the details of his last meeting, while it was fresh in his mind. This would then be transcribed, when he had returned to his London office. She was amused at the thought of an otherwise staid Englishman, running around the streets of Lugano, talking to himself!

He told her how he used to travel by train from Milan, and watch the prosperous Italian passengers, break into a sweat, when they reached the Italian/Swiss border. They had all stored their bulging suitcases, stuffed with Italian Lire banknotes, on the rack above their heads. Then, he told her how he used to see some of them, the following day, paying in their ill-gotten gains across the counters of the Swiss banks that he was visiting. She just nodded; suddenly he remembered that, of course, she knew all about the system of Swiss numbered bank accounts and the flight of money to Switzerland, from all over the world.

The following morning, they took the funicular railway up Monte San Salvatore, Lugano's nearest mountain, to look at the spectacular views of the city, its lake, and the majestic Alps surrounding it, from its summit. In the afternoon, the drive to Locarno on Lake Maggiore, took them only one hour. But while Lake Lugano was a small lake, local to Lugano itself, Lake Maggiore was a large lake stretching for some forty miles. Half in Switzerland and half in Italy, it had a number of towns and cities along its shores. They stayed in Locarno for the rest of the week and over the weekend, Edwards drove them to the charming Italian towns of Stresa and Arona, to see the Italian part of the lake.

They had found a pleasant hotel in Locarno, with a room and balcony overlooking the lake. The weather was almost sub-tropical, with sunny days, mild nights, and a high humidity. They dined on the terrace of the hotel, overlooking the lake and surrounded by the sub-tropical vegetation. It was a relaxing and ideal holiday, but its happy mood was not to last. On their last night, as they lay in bed, looking out at the lake, Muffy started to talk seriously to him.

"My parents are asking me what is going to happen with us?" she said. "They have said that they want a grandchild."

"And what do you want?" asked Edwards.

Muffy looked at him. "I have not told you this before, but I do not want children. I saw too much of the sadness that young children can go through, when I worked in that Children's Home in London."

"But those children were very unfortunate. They were either orphans, abandoned by their parents, or they came from broken homes," protested Edwards. "If a child has both parents and they are living happily together, there should be no problems like that."

"So you would marry me?" asked Muffy suddenly. "And I suppose that we would live in London. I do not think that you could find a job here in Switzerland. You do not speak the language, and it is very difficult for a foreigner to find a job here, even if you were married to a Swiss."

Edwards lay there trying to think of what to say next. He finally came out with "Yes, I would marry you, and you could easily find a job in London."

Muffy nodded. "But I cannot see myself living the rest of my life in England," she said. "My brother cares little for my parents, he is never at home. They are now getting older, and I feel that I must live somewhere close to them."

"But travel is so easy these days" responded Edwards. "We could come and see them, as often as you liked."

"I know," said Muffy. "But it is still a very long way away!"

Edwards had a restless night; he found it difficult to sleep after this traumatic conversation. He knew that Muffy had a self-willed determination in her character, how could he hope to change her mind? Their journey back to Zurich, the following day, was spent mainly in silence. Edwards did try, several times, to restart their conversation of the night before, but Muffy did not seem to want to talk about these matters any further. She seemed to have made her mind up.

After one night's rest at her parents, he was due to start his drive back to London. She came out to see him off in his car. "Thank you for all the wonderful times," was all that she had to say. Edwards had to stop his car, after he had turned the corner of the road, to wipe away the tears from his eyes!

He was not to see her again for some years. The following year was a Leap Year. He did not know it then, but on the extra day of the twenty-ninth of February, he was due to meet his future wife. After they were married, and had bought their first house together, Muffy visited London. She asked if she could come to stay with them for the weekend. Edwards's wife was very understanding, and accepted her visit. They had a friendly time together.

When Edwards's first child, a daughter, was born some years later, Muffy wrote and asked him for a photograph of the baby. Edwards had sent it to her. After a few more years, he would fall out of touch with her. As far as he knew, Muffy never married, or had any children. She continued to live with her parents, in the same flat, in the small town, north of Zurich. But Edwards would never forget his many visits to Switzerland, the spectacular beauty of its mountains and lakes, and the beautiful Swiss girl that he had met, and had sincerely loved.

THE WARRIOR

As told to the Author by M.C., and in his Memory.

"Courage, above all things, is the first quality of a warrior." – Karl von Clausewitz.

1

On an impulse, he stopped the Jeep and sniffed the air. This was the fourth time that he had stopped that morning, and he had already driven some fifty miles from the city's Green Zone. The tarmacked road had now turned into a rough track and the surrounding desert was just scrub. Here and there a few clumps of Saltbush grew and, in between, there was just sand. He turned off the engine and all fell silent. He got out of the Jeep, leaving behind the M4 Carbine, which he was now made to carry by his current American employers. In any case, he much preferred his Russian built AK47. He now kept it under his bed, within easy reach, in case of a night attack. Unless it was constantly cleaned, the M4 had a tendency to jam, just when you needed it. At his hip, in a holster, was the handgun that he also preferred; the Austrian Glock pistol could be relied upon at close quarters, and he was a crack shot with it. For longer work, as a highly trained Sniper himself, he preferred the Russian built modified Dragunov SVD sniper rifle.

He took his high-powered binoculars out of their case and did a careful 360-degree search of the surrounding desert. Nothing stirred, it was strange! There were no sounds of birds, he thought, and no sign of life, of any kind. This was unusual, even in this kind of environment. He returned to the Jeep and took out the spade from the back. He walked slowly away from the vehicle, in ever-increasing circles. He had now finished building the facility, on time, with just a small cost overrun. The most difficult thing had been the importation of specialist equipment. Even for the less important items, he had to visit the airport every time, himself, to claim them. Otherwise, they could just have vanished. Nobody could be trusted these days!

He missed carrying his old AK47, which his men had given him, years ago, in Afghanistan. It had saved his life several times. Over a year ago now, he was being driven with it, across his knees, in the front seat of a Jeep, through a part of the city he sometimes visited. Three amateur insurrectionists had tried to kill him; they had run towards his Jeep firing wildly and inaccurately. He had fired two accurate double rounds into the upper torsos of two of them. They fell immediately, either dead or dying. His well-trained driver had aimed the Jeep at the third would-be assailant, who had fled down a side street in sheer terror. Then his driver had corrected the steering wheel and accelerated away at top speed. He had not even bothered to report the incident. There was too much already happening in the city, to bother the American military authorities with this failed ambush attempt.

Now that the facility had been finished, something had to be found to put into it, and only then could the very careful work begin. He stopped; it seemed only a flat piece of sand, but some instinct that he could not explain, told him something else. He pushed the spade into the ground and started digging. After just over a foot, the spade hit something hard. He dug around it, and then pulled out the buried object. He recognised it as a human leg bone! Carefully he dug around, and in a few minutes he had found some more bones, and then a human skull.

Just to be sure that this was not an isolated burial, he walked on a few yards, and then started digging again. More human bones, he thought. He walked on a few more yards and started his excavation again. This time he found more bones and two skulls. The hot, dry air of the desert had even preserved some of the tissue. He was not an expert, but they looked to him to be male skeletons, and they were probably all young men. In each skull, there was a clean, round hole, where the victim had been shot in the back of the head. Efficiently done, he thought. The victims had been forced to dig their own grave, and then lined up, kneeling in front of it. When they were shot, they toppled easily into the grave, meaning much less work for their executioners. He had found what he was looking for. It was the first, hidden, Mass Grave that had been found in this country.

At least it would have been a quick and merciful death, he thought. The supposed leaders of the resistance would have been dealt with more slowly, using a bayonet, or knives and clubs. Carefully, he took out the instrument and plotted the exact co-ordinates of the site, using the satellite high above. He also carried a satellite phone, but he never used it; nothing was safe in this country. Better to be unobtrusive and quiet, that way you might stay alive.

Out of respect, he reburied the remains that he had found. He could easily find this place again when he came back with his team, accompanied by their heavily armed escort. He went back to the Jeep and carefully wiped his hands on an antiseptic cloth. Quietly, he ate the sandwiches, and drank the amount of liquid he needed, from the thermos box and flask that he had brought with him. Then, before starting the drive back, he got out of the Jeep again and took off the hat that had protected him from the burning, desert sun. He snapped to attention and then bowed his head, to salute the anonymous dead that lay buried all around him.

Back in Baghdad, the next morning, he called together his team. They were mostly Americans, but there were two British, and a Frenchman, as well. Each one had their own particular skills, but each was capable of the detailed forensic analysis that would be needed to secure the evidence that would stand up in a Court of Law, and hopefully convict the guilty members of the old regime. It was not his concern what would happen to them. But he hoped that they would face a short drop, on the end of a rope, for what they had done. Such was the importance put on his team's work, that the human remains that they would painstakingly recover from the site that he had just found, would be flown out by helicopter to the advanced Forensic Facility that had been built, under his close supervision.

He had learnt, early on in life, not to take sides. When he was given a job to do, he would always try, to the very best of his ability, to carry it out. In some cases, maybe his team would be able to identify a particular body; at least that would bring some closure for the grieving family and friends. The one thing he believed in was loyalty to his country, and to his colleagues. His task was now to supervise the recovery of every corpse that they could find, from this first site, and then to go out again and try and find some more Mass Graves which, he was sure, existed at other points in this vast country.

2

He had been born in the valleys of South Wales, the son of a coalminer. Attending the local primary school had been tough but, fortunately, he had always been big for his age, and nobody had tried to bully him. In his secondary school he had played and loved rugby. In the Sixth Form, he had always played in the front row of the scrum, for his School Team. The life of the valleys revolved around rugby, beer, and singing. He had a good bass voice, so he was also inducted into the school choir. When it came to a job, his father wanted him to join the pit, but he did not want to do that. Instead, he loved open spaces, and walking in the hills around his home. It got you away from the smell of the coal dust, which always seemed to permeate everywhere in the narrow, one street, mining town, tucked away in a permanent shadow, between the two large hills.

A family friend was, surprisingly, a policeman. There had always been some suspicion in the valleys, about the police, ever since the General Strike of 1926. He had suggested to the young man that he call and see the Sergeant at their local police station and mention his name. One morning, he did just that. The old

Sergeant looked at the six foot plus, solidly built youngster. "Do you play rugby?" he asked. The young man told him proudly, that he played for his school. "We are looking for a new Prop Forward," said the Sergeant, handing him the Police Force application form. Within two weeks, his application had been accepted, on the condition of course, that he would play for the local Police team.

He remembered well his first working day in the police station, and being fitted out for his new uniform, which he proudly wore. There was not much real crime in the valleys, only the regular fights to break up on Friday and Saturday nights. Friday nights were the worst, as the miners were paid on that day. His rugby skills came in useful in apprehending the more violent, drunken recalcitrant, and taking them away for a night in the cells to sober up by the morning. It was only cleaning the cells out, afterwards, which proved the unpleasant task!

Police training courses followed, and for the first time in his life, he left the valleys and visited England. There he met young Police Constables like himself, from other parts of the country. Some came from the big cities and seemed to look down on "country bumpkins" such as himself. But they did not challenge him, he looked tough, and a glance into his eyes showed that there was both coal and "cold steel" in his background! He soon took and passed his Sergeant examinations, but there was no local vacancy. Suddenly, he was contacted by Police Headquarters. He could get his rank if he volunteered to serve, temporarily, in Northern Ireland. The "Troubles" had started a few years before and, instead of sending in more troops, the Government had decided to deploy some civilian police officers from the mainland to the increasingly unstable Province.

He was prepared for the adventure, and for the risk, so he was soon crossing the Irish Sea and was posted to Londonderry. From there, after only a few months, he was sent to serve in Belfast. He quickly learnt the essentials of keeping safe; you had to rely on your colleagues, and you avoided, rather than provoked, trouble. But if you did have to go in, you went in hard and fast, together, as a team. Inevitably he was taught a lot about weapons, and how to use them, and became a crack shot. Soon others began to notice this young man, who could operate calmly and efficiently under extreme pressure, and under the dangerous urban warfare conditions of Northern Ireland.

The call came to visit a recruitment office, there he was asked if he would like to apply to join the Royal Marines. He applied and was immediately sent for his initial interview and selection tests, which he, of course, passed. Basic physical training followed, and then he was sent on the arduous thirty-two-week Commando

Course, based at Lympstone in Devon. This was considered to be the longest and most arduous military training programme in the world, but he managed to pass it. It was the hardest experience of his life up to then, but, by now, he was already a "trained survivor." Because of his high overall performance, and his native intelligence, he was recommended for promotion, and was sent on additional training courses, to be commissioned as an officer in the Special Boat Service.

With his previous experience of serving in Northern Ireland, he soon found himself back there. He was put in charge of a small, but heavily armed vessel, probing the estuaries and rivers of Northern Ireland for weapons smuggled in for the Irish Republican Army. He excelled at this job and thwarted a number of illegal shipments. But the world was also at war, on other fronts. One morning, he was called in to see his Commanding Officer. "You are off to London tomorrow," he told him. "You have been ordered to attend an interview at the Ministry of Defence, and even I have not been told what it is about."

The daily, slow military transport plane flew him to an airbase in southern England, where he was given overnight accommodation. In the morning, he was given a return railway ticket to London, and a sealed envelope to present at the Ministry Security Desk. His orders were clear: appear in a civilian suit, but carry your Military Pass to identify yourself. Arrive at the Ministry of Defence at least thirty minutes before your appointment, in order to clear Security.

He took a taxi from the railway station to Trafalgar Square. He had never visited London before, so he walked around the Square to view the tall column, with the figure of the great British Admiral on the top, surrounded by its four great sculptured lions. From there, he walked down Whitehall, noting each great government office that he passed at this very centre of British political power. He paused to see the mounted Horse Guards outside the entrance to Horse Guards Parade, and then crossed the wide street. In front of him, was the massive white portal of the Ministry of Defence that he was to visit. He entered and presented his sealed envelope, which was opened by the Security Guard behind his bullet-proof glass window. He was asked for his Military Pass, to identify himself, and was then issued with a Red Pass, which meant that he had to be escorted everywhere, even if he wished to use the lavatory.

He waited for his Security Escort, who took him through two sets of armoured internal entrance doors, and then down a long corridor. He was shown into an outer office, where a pretty secretary was sitting. "He will see you straight away," was all that she said. He was shown into the inner office, and then snapped to attention. Behind a large desk, in full uniform, sat a Brigadier-General. "Sit down," he was ordered. He sat at the desk; in front of him were some papers.

"In front of you are selected, special excerpts from the Official Secrets Act," he was told. "If you are willing, you will please sign them, now, in the place indicated. Until you have done that, we cannot proceed." He signed. "If you ever reveal what I am about to tell you, you will be dishonourably discharged from Her Majesty's Forces, and face a long period in jail," he was then told. "Do you understand?"

"Yes, sir," he replied, promptly.

"I will now make you an offer, which you do not have to accept," the General continued. "Our American allies have asked for our very discrete assistance, in Vietnam. You will be aware that the British Government has officially declined to help them in their war there. But the Prime Minister has now decided to give them some specialist assistance, on a Top-Secret basis. We know your expertise and you, and several other officers, have been carefully selected to be given on loan, to the United States Forces. The Americans are facing the smuggling of weapons by the Viet Cong, up the rivers of South Vietnam. I am led to believe that the prevention of such activity, is your expertise.

Is that correct, and would you be willing to serve in this way under conditions of strict secrecy?"

He left the vast building in a daze. He had accepted, but he would now have to return to Northern Ireland for a week, as ordered, to collect his kit and wind down his current activities. There was to be no explanation, or details, to be given to anybody, including his Commanding Officer. Then, he would be flown back to the mainland again, and then taken to an American air base in England. From there he would be flown out for the long flight to South Vietnam, on a United States Air Force transport aircraft.

3

Edwards sat in the comfortable chair, in the lounge, of the small hotel in West London, where he always met his friend. The hotel was convenient for both of them. It was just off the M25 Motorway, which stretched all around London. His friend could easily reach this hotel on his way down from the Yorkshire Spa town, where he now lived. He could then continue his long drive, on his way to Dover and the Cross Channel Ferry, and then on to the Balkans, usually via Switzerland. They sat together at a small table, with the inevitable large cups of coffee before them.

Edwards had been introduced to this man some fifteen years before. The introduction had come from an American friend of Edwards, who had been visiting London. He knew that this American had served as an agent of one of the American intelligence organisations, clandestinely talent-spotting to help recruit other spies, as well as secretly collecting information from his own highly placed contacts. He had also helped the National Security Council on certain undercover projects; the NSC is the principal forum for American intelligence gathering, reporting directly to the President, and considers all important national security, military, and foreign policy matters. Edwards's American friend had maintained a "cover story." He had indeed been a senior banker at one stage of his life, but now he had his own company specialising in foreign trade. These "cover stories" had given him an excuse to travel widely, while he carried out clandestine operations in various parts of the world.

He was now retired from an active role and lived with his wife in New York. But he still maintained his old intelligence contacts and now, he had too, his own private business interests to take forward. Edwards and he met, occasionally, in London, to discuss mutual opportunities. His American friend was an expert on the British author Charles Dickens and, on one of his trips to London, they had together visited Dickens's former home in Doughty Street, near to the Great Ormond Street Hospital.

It had been a delightful day, and Edwards had been greatly impressed by his American friend's knowledge of this Victorian writer.

"How have you been?" Edwards asked his Welsh friend.

The big man shifted his weight, in the comfortable hotel chair. "Not bad," he replied. "But my tin leg has been giving me some trouble. I think that I will have to go into hospital to get it redone again."

Edwards smiled; he remembered the story that this friend had told him, about how his leg had been repaired after the unfortunate incident in Vietnam. The leg bone had been covered with a steel casing, after the leg had been shattered. "We were assaulting a house," his friend had told him. "We thought that it was a hiding place for the Viet Cong. I throw a grenade in, through the open window, and then kicked down the door."

Immediately, Edwards had understood the problem. "Wrong!" he had said. "First, throw in the grenade, and then wait for it to explode. Only then, kick the door in!"

"You are perfectly right," had been the reply. "My leg took a lot of shrapnel, and that was the end of my time in Vietnam. But the Americans were very grateful to me. I had already trained a lot of their men to carry out the specialist work that they needed. After I was patched up, they flew me to Washington, to carry out the operation on my leg. Then I was introduced to some important people. I was also decorated by the Americans. As a result, I can still get access to top people at the Pentagon, if I need to."

Edwards nodded, he remembered some of the other stories that this man had told him. In late 1979, Russia had invaded Afghanistan to support the "puppet" Communist regime, called the Democratic Republic of Afghanistan, that they had set up some years before in the capital of Kabul. But, in the countryside, various groups were battling against the Soviet Army. The largest grouping was the Mujahideen, who were supported in this "proxy war" between the West and the Soviet Block, by the United States, Saudi Arabia, and Pakistan. Many Afghan civilians were killed, and many more fled their country as refugees, mainly to live in Pakistan and Iran. The Mujahideen had been supplied with arms, equipment, and training, mainly by the Americans and, when they successfully attacked the Russian troops, they stole their arms and equipment as well.

A few years after this war had begun, Edwards's Welsh friend was asked by the Americans to go and train some Mujahideen contingents, in advanced guerrilla warfare techniques. The money had been particularly attractive, and he had agreed to go. He was given a language course in the two Afghan languages of Pashto and Dari, a dialect of the Persian language of Farsi. He was also taught Russian, so that he could interrogate any prisoners that he might take. Then he was flown to Pakistan and finally, in great secrecy, over the border, by helicopter, into Afghanistan, to join his new pupils. He spent a number of happy years in the Afghan mountains, training his native irregulars, and supervising attacks against the Soviet forces. He had never met Osama bin Laden, but he did meet several of the future leaders of what would become the anti-Western organisation, led by bin Laden, called Al-Qaeda, which bin Laden had founded in 1988.

This war was brutal and unrelenting. For a guerrilla group, prisoners were just a burden. They had to be fed and watered, always guarded, and had to be moved around the wild country, as the group regularly moved its base to avoid detection. So, they took few prisoners. Occasionally, he would order the capture of a senior Russian officer or an experienced, older N.C.O., in order to interrogate them. Some of them shot themselves, rather than be captured. When they did not, he found that he could easily obtain some useful information, which he would communicate back to Washington by the discrete means that had been provided to him. Then, unfortunately, he had to dispose of them, mercifully.

Most of the Russian regular troops were young, inexperienced conscripts. Sometimes, his men would capture one alive, particularly if they looked a little effeminate. If this happened, he rounded on them; he made the prisoner turn his back, so that he could not see what was happening. Then he shot them, in the head. Better this merciful death, he thought, than the multiple sodomy and the death by slow torture, that otherwise would have certainly followed. He then told the men who had captured them, in his now almost fluent Pashto, what he would do with the barrels of their own AK47s, before pulling the trigger, if they did this again. This ruthless attitude, was the only way that he could maintain any discipline and, indeed, stay alive himself to maintain the fight against the Soviet enemy.

By mid-1987, the Russians, like the British and others before them, had decided that they could never win this war against these Afghan guerrilla groups. They knew their own country so well, could disappear into its wilderness, and then reappear to successfully attack the Soviet forces, at will. The Russian reformist leader Mikhail Gorbachev had taken over in Moscow and had then started the withdrawal of Soviet troops, which was finally accomplished in February 1989. The pro-Communist

Afghan Government, at last collapsed in 1992, and the Mujahideen groups took over the capital. They eventually became, in a swiftly changing situation, the so-called Taliban government of the country. But intelligent people in Washington had already realised, even before that, that they had created a "Monster!" Edwards's friend had received his secret orders. He did not like them but, he knew, that he had to carry them out.

His guerrilla group was still harrying the Russians, as they started their withdrawal. There was an old road tunnel in the mountains, through which the retreating Russian troops had to go. One night, he had quietly taken the whole stock of explosives that his group held, and had, as he had been trained, laid them carefully inside the tunnel, running the demolition wire out the other side. The following morning, a Russian military column approached the tunnel. He had sent his whole Mujahideen group to follow and destroy them, inside the tunnel, where it would be more difficult for the Russians to escape. Then he took himself to the other end of the tunnel. When he was sure that both the Russians, and his own guerrilla group, were safely inside, he followed his orders and set off the very large explosive charge. The whole tunnel collapsed on to both groups of men, burying them by the sheer weight of the mountain above it. His mission over, he was ferried out that night by helicopter, from the agreed rendezvous.

4

The Yugoslav Wars were a series of ethnic conflicts, which were wars of independence and various insurgencies, fought from 1991 through to 2001. They occurred after the death of the popular leader Josip Broz Tito, in 1980. His death led to the slow, but inevitable, break-up of the former united nation of Communist Yugoslavia. These destructive events were also partly triggered, by the start of the collapse of the Union of Soviet Socialist Republics in 1989, resulting in the formal dissolution of the U.S.S.R. in 1991, and the fall of Communism. But the Balkans already had a long history of violence between the various Christian nationalities living in the historical, six separate and now, increasingly, independent republics, and the Muslim minority. The Muslims lived mainly in the Republic of Bosnia-Herzegovina. The Serbs had always been the dominating force in the Balkans and, as mainly Orthodox Christians, were always closely aligned to the Russians. They had grown to hate the Muslims and they, together with the Croatians, led and supplied a number of insurgent armies to destroy the Muslims, following the declaration of independence by the Republic of Bosnia-Herzegovina.

The war was characterised by indiscriminate shelling of Muslim populated towns and cities, systematic mass rape, and ethnic cleansing through the massacre of large numbers of Muslim civilians. At last, the West intervened, with the targeting of Serb forces by Western air forces, and, finally, the Dayton Accord of November 1995, which finally brought the war to an end. Through the United Nations, a Relief Effort for the population of Bosnia-Herzegovina was started. Aircraft from twenty-one countries took part, and were used to fly in food, medicines, and other supplies, and also to evacuate over 1,300 wounded people. But, on the ground, these supplies had to be distributed to those that needed them, and Edwards's friend was recruited to oversee a large part of this effort. His disciplined organising skills were formidable, and they were fully employed in running convoys of food and medicines, to the places where they were needed.

At first, these convoys had to be protected by a mixed force of foreign troops, and there were many "stand-offs" as the Serbian backed forces tried to stop their distribution. The Relief Effort had to be led with an amount of "Common Sense." Edwards remembered one incident that his friend had told him about. One morning, an American transport plane arrived with a consignment of orange juice, packed into cartons marked "For the Children of Bosnia- Herzegovina." Edwards's friend took one look, and ordered it to either be returned, or dumped into a warehouse. "They did not understand," he later told Edwards. "These children had been eating anything that they could find, including grass, for years. If I gave them this orange juice, of course, they would eagerly drink it. But then they would have the most terrible diarrhoea, which would go on for days, and probably kill a lot of them. I had no medicines available to treat this, and to refuse that shipment, was the only sensible thing that I could do!"

Years later, after the American led invasion of 2003, Edwards's Welsh friend was in Iraq. His stay there included a period of quietly installing an American "listening post", in a remote area of the country, close to the border with Iran. Even there, with the modern technology now available, Edwards was still able to talk to him on a fairly regular basis. "The local Sheik has been very helpful," his friend told him over the satellite communication. "He has provided me with some of his most trusted men, who are protecting me. But I have grown a beard and disguised myself as a local, just in case. My only company out here is my camel. There are no women and I can't help it, but the camel is looking more attractive every day that goes by!"

His next task was to build, equip, and then run for a while, the advanced Crime Scene Investigation facility set up in the specially protected "Green Zone" of Baghdad. Its purpose was to forensically investigate the many crimes that the regime of Saddam Hussein had carried out, including the mass killings of those that had opposed him. The aim was to gather and present the evidence for these crimes, so that senior members of the previous government could be brought to trial and, if found guilty, severely punished.

From Iraq, he was sent to Afghanistan, to supervise the building of a new military compound in a remote part of the country. Although protected with a strong American Army contingent, they still suffered from Taliban and Al- Qaeda attacks. One morning, Edwards contacted his friend; he sounded a little tired. He told Edwards that at four o'clock in the morning, he had been woken up with three incoming Russian-built Scud missiles, which had exploded, fortunately harmlessly, in their encampment. "But it is not all bad news," his friend added. "One on them exploded just where I was going to build the septic tank. Now there is a big enough hole there, and I can save a lot of money not having to dig one!"

Then there were the "Wet Jobs", the words used by the Russian K.G.B. to designate an assassination. As a British "Trained Killer", he was just right for the Americans, who needed a loyal, discrete, unconnected individual. They wanted a deniable, but competent person, to carry out certain tasks that they could ask nobody else to do. Edwards's friend was an ideal candidate: totally reliable, resourceful, and a trained sniper.

He now spoke many languages and could merge himself invisibly into any background. There were a number of these "missions", and for each one he was paid very well, with the money arriving mysteriously into his numbered account, at his Swiss Bank.

He had told Edwards about only two of these tasks, and he was proud of both of them. The first was the elimination of two senior, Columbian drug dealers, who were visiting the Balkans to set up new supply lines for their merchandise. They had been tracked down to a luxury villa, some distance away from Sarajevo. He knew the country well and could speak almost fluent Serbo-Croat. He would have been very happy to do this job without any payment. These evil men were seeking to sell large amounts of their vile products to the very children he had saved from starvation over a decade earlier.

He had taken a local train from the city, and then acquired a bicycle. He was dressed as a local fisherman, and carried his rods in a large bag, slung over his shoulder. Only there were no rods in the bag. Instead, it contained his favourite "tool of the trade", the Russian-made Dragunov SVD sniper rifle, fitted with a powerful telescopic sight. He hid his bicycle and approached the villa on foot. At a distance of 400 yards, he found a small wood to hide in, and surveyed the scene through the telescopic sight. The two criminals were sitting beside the swimming pool, surrounded by a number of scantily clad local girls.

They were too relaxed, and there was no sign of any bodyguards. His first shot hit one of them in the head. The other turned to flee, and he shot him twice in the back. All the girls were unharmed, but they fled in terror. He then calmly collected his bicycle and cycled back to the local railway station. "I had a very good day's fishing, but I put them all back," he told the locals, who asked him about his day out, on the train back to the city.

The second mission he imparted to Edwards was his last of this type. It took him to Eastern Ukraine, an area now being fought over between the Armed Forces of the new Republic of the Ukraine, and Russian-backed rebels. He had been told that a woman had attached herself to the latter, and was already notorious for her activities against the West. Born in Northern Ireland, as a teenager, she had converted to Islam. Her first husband had blown himself up on a London Tube train. She eventually moved to East Africa and worked with several terrorist movements there. Several police forces were still searching for her, in regard to the deaths of over four hundred people! This time he acquired a motorbike for transport and dressed himself in the military fatigues favoured by the rebels. He did not bother to hide his Russian made weapon, after all he was a sniper, and he spoke fluent Russian, if challenged. Fortunately for him, the Ukrainian Government Forces had, temporarily, retreated, after the rebels had won some hard-fought victories.

It was very efficiently done. He parked his motorbike on a country lane, close to the rebel camp where, he had been told, the woman was trying to assist the rebels with her terrorist experience. There was even a low wall he could hide behind. He soon spotted her through his powerful binoculars, she was easy enough to identify. He had been given her exact height and build, and she was the only person in the camp wearing a full burka! She was walking around the camp, talking to the guerrillas. A single shot to the head was sufficient, and she fell down dead. Before the camp even woke up to what had happened, he was already speeding away on his motorcycle.

5

Like us all, even Warriors age. They are soon too old to carry out their duties. Sometimes, they can retire gracefully and rest, at last, in peace. His last mission was one of attempted mercy. He told Edwards that three men from the Balkans had been captured in Libya, by an Islamic State terrorist group, operating there. Ever since the deposing and killing of its leader, Muammar Gaddafi, this country had been in a state of chaos, with competing armed factions claiming to control certain parts of it. With the permission of the particular Libyan "Government", then in charge at Benghazi, an American Air Force transport plane had landed with a contingent of U.S. Navy SEALs on board. He had been picked up in England, when they had landed to refuel at a U.S. Air Force base. By now, he spoke both Arabic and Serbo-Croat fluently. His role was to act as a negotiator, if needed, and if the American Special Forces managed to rescue the hostages, to make sure that they were looked after properly.

He stayed behind, with the small number of men left to guard the aircraft. In case the plane was attacked, he found himself cover in a bomb crater, to the side of the isolated runway and, as the nights can be cold in the desert, slept in his warm sleeping bag. Unfortunately, the mission was a failure, and he was never called upon to help. The majority of the Americans had gone off to first reconnoitre the terrorists' camp. But they were spotted, and there was a savage firefight. The three hostages were killed by the Muslim extremists, and the Americans killed at least six of them in return, without taking any casualties on their side. But he may well have been a casualty of this or, indeed, past military actions.

After his return to England, he began to feel ill. He went to his doctor, who had sent him to his local hospital for some tests.

They all came back with negative results. Soon he was so ill, that he had to be taken into hospital. Many more tests followed, but none of his doctors could identify what he was suffering from. He was given a total blood transfusion and recovered enough to be discharged from hospital. But soon he was back in hospital again. More tests took place, but his illness proved to be a complete mystery to the National Health Service.

Edwards kept track of what was happening to his friend; he had lost a lot of weight and was becoming weaker. The last time Edwards had telephoned him, was to enquire how he was? "You are the only one who cares," his friend had said to him, gratefully. The last message that Edwards received, was a text wishing Edwards a "Merry Christmas", which he had replied to in a similar vein. Then there was silence. Edwards tried to contact him many times, but his mobile and email had stopped working. At last, Edwards had, unfortunately, to assume the worst. He had heard nothing more from, or about, the "Warrior", and he had no way of finding out about him. He had lived alone, without a family, and with few friends and acquaintances.

Edwards had heard stories of the untested cocktail of drugs administered to the Allied troops who had fought in the First Gulf War, after Iraq had invaded Kuwait in 1990. These drugs were, supposedly, to help to protect them against the chemical and bacteriological weapons that, it had been claimed by the West, Saddam Hussein possessed. In later life, a number of these men started to suffer serious illnesses which no doctor could explain, and no medical tests could help diagnose. Only now are some doctors, who have the necessary experience, beginning to recognise the long-term effects of what was once administered to these soldiers, to try and protect them. His friend had not told him about his experiences in that war, but Edwards had to assume that, in some way, he had taken part in it, and he could well have been given doses of these largely untested drugs.

Or was it something worse than that? Edwards's friend was now too old to be of further use but, unfortunately, he just knew too much! There are a number of chemical compounds made around the world, that can defy recognition by medical science. Some can also be "engineered" so that their effects are delayed. Could one of these have, somehow, been administered on a lonely airfield in the dead of night, in a lawless country? A friendly cup of coffee given, perhaps, to a man who was trying to keep warm in his sleeping bag? An American Special Forces operative, who had perhaps another agenda, than just helping to rescue three men, from the clutches of the Islamic State?

Edwards would never know, but he had his suspicions. The military are, after all, just the servants of the State. Warriors need to be protected, so that they can fight efficiently. But, once they become too old, they are no longer of any use. If they can, perhaps, also cause embarrassment, then does the State really care any longer about what might happen to them?

SPEED BOATS

"Americans are the Great Satan, the wounded snake."
– Grand Ayatollah Ruhollah Khomeini.

1

Edwards was instantly fully awake. It was the morning of an ordinary working day in the early 1980s. He had just been dozing, listening to the six o'clock morning B.B.C World Service news on his bedside clock radio. He was awakened by this excellent international news program, every morning at the same time, during his working week, and even at the weekends. He had to listen to it because he dealt with the financial affairs of a group of major construction companies who were already working, or had potential projects, in so many different countries around the world.

But that morning, one particular item on this news program, had prompted him to get quickly out of bed and begin to prepare to go to work. Edwards had learnt, early in his time within this international group, that priority had to always be given to people who had been deployed overseas, and who, sometimes, had to face difficult, or even dangerous, situations.

He quickly ate his two wheat cereal biscuits as usual, drank his cup of tea, and then made his first strong coffee of the day. He would drink that after he had shaved and showered and got dressed, just before he left in his company car, to drive to his office in West London. It was a tiresome drive most mornings, but his company car was free, as was his petrol. He was only taxed a small amount on its supposed value, and there was really no choice for him between driving to work, where he also had a free car parking space, and trying to get to work on a series of expensive and crowded underground trains, that often had an unreliable service.

His office was high up above the flyover taking the traffic from central London, past Heathrow Airport, and then out to the west. As soon as he arrived, his Personal Assistant Liz brought him his second steaming mug of coffee of the day. He made the telephone call as soon as he thought it would be answered. He knew that it was pointless to make the call, until this time. The Foreign Office civil servant that he wanted to speak to, travelled in by underground train, and would not arrive in his office before then.

At last, he made the call, and managed to get hold of the man he needed in the Foreign Office's Middle Eastern department. "Have you revised your advice for British Citizens in Iran?" he asked. The reply came back in the negative. "The B.B.C. World Service News, at six o'clock this morning, had a relevant item," Edwards reported. "They said that Radio Tehran was saying that the country was full of Western spies, and that they must be hunted down and eliminated. Have you heard of that report?" He was nonplus; why was the Foreign Office so often behind with the news? He received a promise to investigate the situation immediately, and to call him back.

Edwards had an early morning meeting in the headquarters building of his group of companies in Central London, and now he had to leave his office. He had informed the civil servant of that fact. He left, and took an underground train to the station close to the Group's headquarters building. It was near to one of the famous London squares, which provided a green space, bordered by trees, in the heart of London. He showed his pass to the man behind the security desk at the main door, and then took the lift up to the large, second floor room, where his meeting was to take place. The meeting had been in progress for about thirty minutes, when a secretary came in: "There is a very urgent call from the Foreign Office for you," she whispered into Edwards's ear.

Edwards knew that the lives of nine men, could now well depend on what he did next! He stood up, and gave his excuses to the chairman of the meeting. Outside the room, he asked the secretary to transfer the call to one of the nearby empty offices, went in, and closed the door behind him. The man at the Foreign Office apologised, they had now decided to revise their advice to British Citizens in Iran.

"What is your advice now please?" asked Edwards.

"We are now advising all British Citizens to leave the Islamic Republic of Iran, by the fastest possible means!" came the official reply.

Edwards politely thanked the official and put the telephone down. He thought for a moment, today was a Friday. Immediate action was required, that day! He was the man who would have to make this decision, now. After all, he knew more about the situation than anyone else. If he approached any of his group directors, there would be endless delay, and then probably they would make the wrong decision, after days of discussion between them.

He dialled the internal number for the Head of the Group's Personnel Department and reported to him what he had just heard from the Foreign Office. "Please send a very urgent telex to the office in Bandar Abbas and include the agreed coded phrase for them all to pull out of the country immediately," he said. He was assured that this would be done within the hour.

Edwards thought for a minute; he had several more things that he must do. He consulted his pocket diary that had some useful telephone numbers in it. He dialled an outside number which connected to the subsidiary company, within his group, who were actually responsible for the work that was being carried out in Iran. He identified himself, and asked to speak to their Managing Director, very urgently. He was put through, and told this man about the new Foreign Office advice, and what he had done as a result. The Managing Director agreed with his decision, and kindly said that he would support Edwards if any of his group directors criticised him for the decision that he had made.

Edwards then dialled another outside number. This call went through to the office of the Head of the Middle East section of the British Government's Export Credits Guarantee Department. He was well known to that organisation, and the secretary that answered his call put him through straight away. He reported to this senior civil servant what the Foreign Office had just said, and what, as a result, he had decided to do.

2

The Export Credits Guarantee Department was the then British Government organisation that supported British companies to export overseas. It provided its guarantee to approved banks, to support the overseas sale of British goods and services, by means of these banks making long-term loans available to foreign governments, at attractive interest rates. Every developed country had its own Export Credit organisation which, in a similar way, supported their own national companies, and their country's exports overseas. But E.C.G.D., as it was known, was also an insurance company. For an insurance premium, which the British company paid, this organisation would insure that the company would receive the payments due to it under an approved "cash contract", as compared to a "credit contact", where a loan by a British bank had been made.

Edwards's employer had a cash contract with the Iranian Government, and Edwards, sometime before, had taken out the appropriate insurance cover with E.C.G.D. and arranged for the payment of the insurance premium. Since he had just prevented the contract's completion, Edwards had to tell his insurance company immediately of his decision, and why he had decided to make it. E.C.G.D. also covered the political, as well as the financial, risks of operating overseas and he knew that, now, he would have to submit a claim under the terms of their complex insurance policy. There would then be long months of negotiation before, he hoped, the full amount that his company would claim, would be paid out.

The Islamic Republic of Iran had been created after rioting on the streets of Iran in April 1979, in which nearly three thousand Iranians had been killed. Its then autocratic ruler, the Shah of Iran, had left his country and gone into exile in Egypt, in the January of that year. He had left the country in the hands of a Regency Council. But this was quickly dissolved, later that month. Grand Ayatollah Khomeini returned to Iran, from his exile in Paris, on the first of February, and quickly took control of what, he then declared to be, an Islamic Revolution. The Iranian Armed Forces were then persuaded to revoke their allegiance to the Shah, and Khomeini set about quickly establishing a new theocracy.

Although Iran, under the Shah's rule, was becoming an increasingly advanced, secular state, Khomeini imposed a new, harsh, religious regime. He used religion, as it has always been used, to establish firm social control, increasing military efficiency by promising warriors paradise if they died in God's cause, and maintaining the subjugation of women. While Iran maintained the façade of democracy, with free elections, a President, a Prime

Minister, and a government through elected politicians, there was no doubt where the real power actually lay. The new Constitution of December 1979 made clear that all democratic procedures and rights were subordinated to the Guardian Council of senior clerics, and the Supreme Leader, the Grand Ayatollah, had the final word on what would actually happen in the country.

Iran quickly became anti-Western, partly because of its recent history. The Shah's father had seized power in a coup d'état in 1925, but was then deposed by Allied Forces in 1941, when he refused to get rid of the Germans, who ran the Iranian railway system. He was forced into exile, and his son was installed by the Western Forces, as the new Shah. But then he also had to flee the country in 1953, when a popular, left-wing Prime Minister Mohammed Mossadegh, was elected. Fearful that they would lose their control over the Iranian oil reserves, the American and British intelligence agencies then engineered a plot to oust him and paid for pro-Shah riots to take place in Iran. One part of the Iranian Army turned against Mossadegh, and he was arrested and imprisoned until his death in 1967. The Shah returned to power but, over the following years, his regime had been seen as becoming increasingly corrupt, extravagant, and out of touch with the ordinary people.

Given this troubled history of intervention, Khomeini now targeted the West as constantly interfering in Iranian affairs, and so, against his new Islamic Republic. In November 1979, the American Embassy in Tehran was invaded by a mob, controlled by the new Islamic Government, and fifty-two American diplomats and citizens were then captured and held hostage, until they were finally released in January 1981. To bolster the internal support for his theocratic regime, Khomeini set up the Islamic Revolutionary Guard Corps, as part of the Armed Forces. But it reported directly to the Supreme Leader and was specifically formed to protect the new Islamic Republic from its foreign enemies, and from internal 'deviant movements' and foreign spies, who, it was believed, would seek to undermine the new theocratic regime.

3

Edwards was well aware of this recent history of Iran. It was his job to be so, especially as one of the construction companies he looked after now had a team of nine men located at Bandar Abbas, the Iranian port on the Strait of Hormuz. A year before, this company had signed a cash contract to provide the material for, and to construct, a new ship lift at this port. The ship lift itself was a large, metal cradle, capable of lifting small and even medium sized vessels out of the water, to carry out essential maintenance and repairs. The large, steel pieces needed to construct the ship lift, were made at the company's works in England, and then shipped to Iran. There they were put together by this British team, with the help of some local labour, and then carefully erected on the site designated by the Iranian Port Authorities.

Edwards had met with the company's Project Manager, both before he left for Iran, and when he had returned to England for a holiday. What he had told Edwards had raised some concern in his mind, and Edwards had insisted that the Project Manager should set up a series of agreed coded sentences with the Personnel Department, so that certain vital messages could be sent in secret by telex message. Edwards knew that these telex messages would always be read by the Iranian intelligence organisation.

During the negotiation for this contract, Edwards had received a telephone call from the Marketing Director of the company concerned, who was in Tehran. The man stupidly began to talk about the greedy people "who were crawling out of the woodwork, asking for bribes, to award the contract!" Edwards quickly cut him short as the man was very busy digging his own grave!

"You realise that there are four intelligence agencies listening to this call?" he had said.

That had, finally, shut the Marketing Director up. Because of what he knew about the likely international position, Edwards had meant that the British, American, Russian, and Iranian intelligence agencies would have, almost certainly, being intercepting all such calls between Iran and the outside world.

Edwards liked the Project Manager, who had been appointed to lead this Iranian contract in Bandar Abbas. For an engineer, he had a wide variety of interests, including playing a number of musical instruments. He was widely read, and carried out a variety of voluntary charitable work when he was at home back in England. He was an unmarried man with no children, and therefore was suited to be able to concentrate fully on getting this construction project done, in what was certainly, a difficult and potentially dangerous situation.

On his return to Britain for a short holiday, he had come to see Edwards to advise him of the physical situation of his British team in Bandar Abbas. "We are working out of a couple of converted containers," he had said. "They are located alongside where we are building the ship lift, in one of the dock basins in the port. Next door to us, in the adjoining basin, the Revolutionary Guards keep their main fleet of speed boats. They are all heavily armed, and they go out to patrol the Strait of Hormuz!"

Edwards was immediately worried as he knew the importance of the Strait of Hormuz. The Strait lay between the coast of Iran and the Arabian Peninsula. At the narrowest point they were only twenty-one nautical miles wide. All the oil and gas exports from the Arabian Gulf were sailing, in tankers, through the Strait of Hormuz. If the Iranians ever wanted to cause real trouble, they would not need to block the Strait. All they had to do was to attack just one oil tanker with say, a rocket-propelled grenade, and the vital oil and gas supplies to the West would, at once, be stopped. Every insurance company in the world would refuse to insure these cargos, and the Western governments would have to take over all the risks.

"I hope that you do not have a pair of binoculars?" he had asked the Project Manager.

"Yes I do," was the reply. "I keep them in my office."

"For goodness sake!" said Edwards. "Make sure that you take them back to your flat as soon as you get back. If the Revolutionary Guards decide one day, to search your offices, they will find them. Then they will accuse you of spying on the movements of their fleet of armed speed boats!"

Some two weeks after Edwards had given his order to evacuate the British team from Bandar Abbas, the Project Manager came to see him back in London. "I have just come to thank you," he said. "I understand that it was you who gave the order for us to return home. I doubt if any of our Directors would have bothered to extract us so promptly."

"I thought that it was necessary once I heard details of the broadcast from Radio Tehran, about Western spies being in the country," replied Edwards. "Then, the Foreign Office changed its advice, about British Citizens staying there."

The Project Manager looked at him thoughtfully. "We did not work on Fridays, out of respect for our Muslim neighbours," he said. "So I got the coded message on Saturday morning, when we returned to the site. I spent the rest of that weekend getting us all Exit Visas," he went on. "It involved a very large bribe, paid to various Iranian officials. Then I sent my men out, in groups of two, so as to avoid suspicion. They each took the daily flight from Tehran that lands, to pick up more passengers, at Bandar Abbas. It then goes on to Dubai. I took each group to the local airport myself, and paid for their tickets from our cash float, over the four days needed."

Edwards nodded in agreement with this man's actions, but then he went on: "Over the first two days, I evacuated those with wives and small children at home. Then I sent the younger, single men out, and finally, the older ones. When they had all left, on the Friday, I took the same flight out by myself."

"Just like a ship's Captain, abandoning his ship!" Edwards said, smiling. He was now in total admiration of this man, whose cool and calm actions, had probably saved his team from some terrible fate.

But nothing had prepared Edwards for what this man was about to say next. He looked at Edwards. "Your decision, to pull us all out, was correct," he said. "On the Monday that we had started on this evacuation, the rest of us that were left had driven to the site as normal. We did not want anybody to suspect anything. Then we began to realise that something was very wrong. At the main entrance to the port complex, the street is lit, at night, by twelve, high lamp posts. That morning, from each lamp post, was hanging, by the neck, a human body!"

Edwards said nothing; he just gasped in horror!

A BRIDGE TOO FAR

"Judgement comes from experience and experience comes from bad judgement" – Simon Bolivar.

1

Edwards stared, rather moodily, out of the aircraft window next to his comfortable business class seat. It was the middle of the 1980's. He was tired; it had been a long and difficult journey, and he had not been able to sleep. He was just jaded with flying and travelling, and he felt that he had had enough of it all, over the last few years. There had been no direct flights to his destination and the Travel Agent, who looked after the group of construction companies that he worked for, had routed him through New York. The morning flight from London had been late landing, and Edwards had been growing increasingly worried that he would miss his vital connection.

Then he had discovered that the egocentric Americans, did not provide any transit facilities. They assumed that everyone arriving would want to visit their beloved country! So Edwards had had to join the long, slowly-moving queue for Immigration. Fortunately, he had a multi-entry United States Visa; the Immigration Official, when he had finally reached him, had been quite quick. As he handed Edwards back his British Passport, he had asked "How long will you be staying in the United States, sir?"

Edwards quickly looked at his watch. "About one hour," he had replied.

During his two flights, instead of being able to sleep, his mind had been working hard on planning out the next few days. He saw them as just another of his "Missions Impossible." During his time looking after the financial affairs of many complex projects for his employers, a major, international construction group, he had been given a number of these. He used to say hopefully to some of his colleagues who would listen, and then usually smile at him: "Miracles can be done in a day. The impossible usually takes a little longer."

Outside there was complete darkness; he sensed that they were descending, and would soon be coming into land. They must be over the Caribbean as there were no lights of any kind, even from passing ships. The aircraft's wheels came down. Suddenly, he saw the shape of land and some lights below, then they touched down with a gentle bump. The aircraft came to a complete stop, and the door was opened. As he descended the stairs to the ground, the heat and the very high humidity hit him like a wall. He could stand up to this heat, after all, he was an Englishman! But it was the humidity that, finally, got to you.

He remembered one day in New York, when he was visiting at the end of his time as a student. It had been high summer, and outside it was 95 degrees Fahrenheit, and 95 per cent humidity. For some reason, he had chosen that very day to climb up inside the Statue of Liberty, a gift from the people of France to the United States, made out of copper. When he had arrived back down, on the ground of the small island on which this great statue stood, his clothes had been drenched in his own sweat.

He passed through Immigration quickly, and then Customs. He had no case to collect; everything he needed was in his carry-on bag which he had stored above his aeroplane seat. He found a taxi, and gave the driver the name of his hotel. The taxi was not air-conditioned, but all its windows were open. Once they were out of the airport, they joined a six-lane motorway and started the long climb into the mountains, to the capital city of this South American country.

Edwards looked out of the car window. Above him, on the steep slopes on either side of the motorway, twinkled the multiple lights of the many favelas. These were the shanty towns, where the poor lived; they were desperate to live close to the city as that was where some work could, perhaps, be found. It was a "white-knuckle ride" as there seemed to be no Highway Code in this country. Drivers were just competing with each other to overtake, in the fastest and most dangerous way possible. Edwards noticed that the fastest-moving line of traffic was actually on what should have been the hard shoulder! The sheer volume of traffic had turned what should have been a six-lane motorway, into an eight-lane "Dice with Death!"

Higher and higher they climbed, and as they did so, the temperature and the humidity fell sharply. Amazingly, he arrived safely at his five-star, but rather run-down hotel, in the centre of Caracas. It seemed to be cold, compared to the heat of the coast far down below the mountains, where the airport stood. He was on a two-day mission: there was a new major bridge to be built over the River Orinoco, deep in the heart of Venezuela. The bridge building company, which was one of the companies he looked after in his construction group, wanted to help in its construction.

The project had been brought to them by the owner of a Venezuelan construction company which had its own steel fabrication works on the banks of the river, not far from the planned site of the new bridge. Because of his connections into the Venezuelan government, this man had won the contract to build this new project, despite the fact that he was totally incapable of designing, or undertaking the complex construction work needed, for such a major bridge.

Edwards had met this man in London. He had been introduced to him by the Scottish Marketing Director of their successful bridge building company, and they had gone out for lunch together. "We won't take too much time over it," the Scotsman had muttered to Edwards. "He treats lunch or dinner, not as an enjoyable social occasion, but merely as a refuelling stop!"

The Venezuelan, indeed, seemed to be a "driven man". He talked incessantly about business between gulping his food down. Fortunately, he spoke good English, although his parents had been Dutch and had settled in Venezuela before he had been born. Most of the fabricated steel, for the new bridge, would come from this man's works. But what Edwards was interested in, was how their British company would be paid for the design work, making some of the more complex components, and all the other work that they would have to do to fit the fabricated steel together? Then they would actually have to carefully erect the new bridge, over the broad river, at the planned site.

He questioned the Venezuelan about this; it became clear that they would be paid through his company, as a sub-contractor, once he had been paid by the Venezuelan Government. But, Edwards was unhappy with this route: not only were they taking a risk on the Venezuelan Government paying this man's company what was due to him, but they were also taking the risk that he would then pay on to them, what they were specifically due for their work.

"What we need, is to be a Nominated Sub-Contractor, so that the government can pay us directly," he told him, rather uncertain that this man might take this request as an insult.

But, fortunately, the man understood Edwards's concern. "You will have to visit the Ministry of Public Works, and seek their permission for this direct payment," he told Edwards. "Then, since everything is controlled by the Ministry of Finance, you will have to go and get their permission too. But I will help you. I have good contacts in both Ministries that you can meet, and who will help." He winked at Edwards. "What is good for you is that they all speak good English," he added. Then he grinned. "Because, I don't think that you speak good Spanish!" Edwards was pleased that he had found a route to go forward on this problem of securing payments for his company.

At this point, the Marketing Director excused himself and left, he had another meeting back at the office. It was then that the

Venezuelan dropped the bombshell! "But of course, for this project, the money is not coming from Venezuela. It is coming from the Government of Panama, as aid money." Edwards's jaw dropped open. He knew that Venezuela had the largest oil reserves in the World, even bigger than the oil reserves of Saudi Arabia. The country was producing and exporting oil from its many wells around its Maracaibo Basin region. Why was a relatively poor country such as Panama, providing aid money to a rich country like Venezuela, to build a new bridge over the River Orinoco? He asked the Venezuelan that very question.

The man looked at him. "Let us put it this way," he said. "Yes, my country has a large oil reserve and it is producing a lot of oil. Petrol is very cheap for the population in Venezuela. A lot of oil is also exported, but, somehow, a lot of the money that comes in from that oil, seems to disappear. Somehow, a lot of it finds its way into private bank accounts in Panama. The people that have it there, may have a conscience or, maybe, they are told that some of it must come back to Venezuela, so that they can keep on taking out the money to Panama." His eyebrows shot up. "I think that you understand?" he said.

Edwards did understand, this was a highly corrupt system whereby some rich and powerful people could become even more rich and powerful. But they had to follow certain rules, so that this "gravy train" of money paid to them, could go on. The Venezuelan continued: "Then there are certain people, in Panama, who receive a portion of the money, who are prepared to say that the money coming back is actually aid money from Panama."

After the lunch, the Venezuelan returned to his nearby hotel, to "have his Siesta", as he put it. Edwards went back to the office, and there he found the Marketing Director, and tackled him on the difficult problem that he now had. He told him everything that he had heard. "Do we really want to get involved in this project, which is funded by corruption?" he asked.

The Scotsman did not hesitate. "If it is work for us, I don't care," he replied. "Besides, some of these people seem to be returning some of the money back, to benefit their own country," he added. "Who are we to judge them?"

Edwards was appalled by this attitude. He asked for a meeting with the Finance Director he reported to, and told him what he had learnt about the project and how it was to be paid for. The Finance Director consulted with the Managing Director of the bridge building company, who said, nevertheless, that he wanted to go ahead with the project. It did not matter how it would be financed. Venezuela needed the project as a strategic bridge over that river, and his company was able to help in that, and the company needed the business.

2

So it was that Edwards was sent, rather unwillingly, to Caracas. He was very uncertain as to how he should handle this visit, but he knew that while he was there, he had to treat this project as a legitimate one. If he showed that he knew how it was really financed, something unpleasant might happen to him. He might, just, not be able to return home alive!

He had taken up the offer that the Venezuelan businessman had made to him; the next morning he was sitting in the Ministry of Public Works, with the two civil servants that he had suggested that Edwards should meet. As he had said, they both spoke good English. He explained to them his idea, that the company that he represented should become a Nominated Sub-Contractor recognised by the Venezuelan Government, under the main contract to build the new bridge. Then, they would need their government to pay his company directly for the work that they had done. That work would be certified, as having actually been done, by an independent engineer who would be appointed for this purpose, so that the government's money would be fully protected.

Edwards then told them how he thought that it was essential for their government to use the expertise of his group, to work together with the Venezuelan company, to get this new bridge to be properly completed. "If you cannot agree to this arrangement for my company, and pay us directly, we, unfortunately, will not be able to help you to complete this contract," he concluded. The two civil servants understood him, and asked him some questions, which he hoped that he answered correctly. Then they said that they were happy to recommend this arrangement to their Minister, but that he now had to visit the Ministry of Finance, as their approval would also be required.

Edwards had expected this and he told them that, the following day, he would be meeting with an official of the Ministry of Finance, and gave them his name so that they could then contact him after Edwards's meeting. He mentioned that this man, too, had been recommended to him by the owner of the Venezuelan company that Edwards had met in London. The two civil servants smiled and nodded, they said that they knew the owner of the company well, and that Edwards was going to meet the right man in the other Ministry.

The next morning, he was at the Ministry of Finance. He was kept waiting for well over an hour, to meet the official that he needed to see. At last, he was shown into the man's room. From the size of the room and its lavish decoration, he realised that he was meeting a senior official of the Ministry of Finance. The man was charming as he shook Edwards's hand. "I am so sorry to have kept you waiting," he said, in a perfect English accent.

"Where did you learn to speak such good English?" asked Edwards, somewhat intrigued.

The man laughed. "I was sent, by my father, to one of your peculiar English institutions," he said. "It was called a Public School, but, as you will know, those kinds of schools are actually private!"

Edwards told him about his discussions at the Ministry of Public Works the previous day, and then asked him if the Ministry of Finance could also approve of his suggestion as, he understood, that they too had to agree to the status of his company as a Nominated Sub-Contractor. It would also be necessary to pay his company directly, for the work that they were going to do. "I am afraid that it is not as easy as that," the man replied. "I can probably get that request approved by my Minister, but then you will have to take that decision to the Ministry of Finance in Panama City. They will then have to approve it, too. After all, they are supplying the money to pay for this project."

"Have they confirmed that the funds are available?" asked Edwards.

"Yes," came the reply. "We would not have started on the process of asking your main contractor for his bid, if they had not done that. But I must tell you that Panama has confirmed that the money was available for previous projects, but then it has never materialised."

Maybe it was his perfect English accent, but Edwards had begun to feel that he could trust this man. "I must tell you," he said, "that we may have to ask for an increase in the price that the main contractor has submitted, because, of course, he did not include the cost of the work that we will supply."

The official laughed, "We expected that anyway," he said. "That means, of course, that we will have to explain to the Panamanians that we will need some more money. If you can let me know what the new total cost of the project will now be, I will ask my Minister to write a letter to his counterparty in Panama, with this information, asking if the additional funds can now be made available? But you will understand that this will be a private letter. When the letter is ready, I will let you know. You can then come to collect it, and take it personally to Panama yourself. I will provide you with the name of the right person to deliver it to there, and inform them that you are coming."

Edwards thanked the official most warmly; he had been very helpful in what he had promised to do. Edwards returned to his hotel to send a telex message to the Marketing Director that he must have a new estimate of the price of the bridge, to include a full breakdown of the cost of all the work that his company would have to do. He would need that within the next couple of days. Then he checked out of his hotel, and took a taxi, this time down the "Dice with Death", to the airport. He was booked on the return flight to New York, late that evening. Again, he would have to endure the long, late-night queue for American Immigration, and then, hopefully, a prompt morning flight to return to London.

Back in the office a few days later, Edwards received the new increased price for the project from the Marketing Director of the bridge building company, within his group. He sent this new amount, with a detailed explanation and breakdown of what these increased costs consisted of, by a telex message to the Ministry of Finance official. He requested that he kindly inform his colleagues at the Ministry of Public Works, of these changes. A few weeks later, the message came back from Caracas, to Edwards, that the letter from the Minister of Finance was ready for his collection.

3

This time, for Edwards, it was a more relaxed trip. First, he demanded from the Travel Agency, that they book him via a European airport that had proper Transit Facilities, and that had a direct flight to Caracas. He thought that he now knew better, what to expect, when he arrived. This time he flew to Madrid, and then took a direct flight back to the steamy airport. Then there was the interesting, but dangerous, taxi ride up into the mountains, to the capital city of Venezuela.

After a restful night at the same hotel, he met the "Public Schoolboy" again, at the Ministry of Finance. "Here is the letter," he said, handing over a sealed envelope, bearing no name or address, and then a piece of paper. "For you, here is an English translation that I have made, of what it says inside." He then handed Edwards another piece of paper. "Here is the name and address of the person you are to meet, in Panama City. I have informed him that you will arrive there tomorrow morning, and he will see you at three o'clock tomorrow afternoon. Please give him the sealed envelope, as he is a representative of their Minister of Finance."

Edwards read through the translation carefully, it was addressed to the Minister of Finance in Panama City. It was an excellent letter, he decided, and it said everything that needed to be said. Over a coffee, they then chatted for an hour about England. Unusually, for a Venezuelan, he had a real knowledge of cricket! As he was about to leave, Edwards decided that he must ask a question that had really been troubling him. "Why is this letter not being sent by normal Diplomatic Channels, via your Embassy, in Panama City?" he asked.

The "Public Schoolboy" paused then he said: "You will understand that this is a private letter. The man in Panama you will deliver it to, may decide to hand it to the President of Panama first. He is also well aware of this project.

By now, Edwards knew what he was really being told! The President of Panama might also have a "personal interest" in this project, as well as the Minister of Finance. Having finished his meeting, Edwards decided that he would walk back to his hotel; it was a pleasant, dry, and sunny day.

Somehow, he felt safe in this city, but he could see some real poverty around him. Those that were white appeared to be in a small minority among the people he saw; they were probably of Spanish descent and were well-dressed and looked prosperous.

But, the majority of the people that he saw were not white, shabbily-dressed and really looked poor. This group were surely descended from the original inhabitants of the country. But among them, there were some well-dressed people of native blood that Edwards could not help noticing; they were mainly young and very attractive women!

The next morning he arrived, on the two hour fight, from Caracas to Panama City. As he got off the aircraft, he was virtually overwhelmed with the heat and humidity. It was far worse even, than the weather at Caracas Airport. Panama seemed to have an unhealthy climate; no wonder that so many people had died digging the Panama Canal, Edwards thought! He was very grateful that there was an air-conditioned taxi available at the airport, to take him to the address where he was expected. It turned out to be a small, smart, office block, completely occupied by a firm of lawyers.

There he was politely received, and conducted into the plush office of the Senior Legal Partner. The man was immaculately dressed, in a three-piece suit, shirt and matching tie, with burnished black shoes. He oozed charm itself! He asked his pretty secretary to bring Edwards anything that he wanted. Edwards asked for a coffee, then handed over the sealed, unaddressed letter that he had been given. "I think that you know what to do with this," he said.

"Of course," replied the lawyer. "We will first have to consult with our clients. Then, we will decide which is the best route to use to approach our Government, with this request. You must leave matters with us, for a while. When I have a final solution, I will contact the gentleman who you have met at the Ministry of Finance in Caracas."

Having carried out his task, Edwards wanted to leave quickly. But the lawyer insisted on getting his secretary to call for a taxi to take Edwards to his hotel. The hotel was run-down, and the air conditioning, in Edwards's room, did not work properly. He complained at the reception desk, but nothing was done. That evening, he decided to risk the hotel's restaurant, and had a lonely dinner all by himself. "Such are the delights of international business," he thought, as he ate his meal. He had an uncomfortable night, lying on top of the bed, and trying to sleep in the clinging heat. The next morning he thankfully checked out, took a taxi to the airport, then a direct flight back to London.

Back in the office, the weeks went by with no message from Caracas. He sent a reminder telex to the "Public Schoolboy" in the Venezuelan Ministry of Finance. Still there was no reply. He met with the Finance Director, who he reported to, so that they could discuss the project. The man was an accountant by background, but had many years of experience of working for the group, and looking after all the construction companies within it.

"I feel that I will have to visit Caracas," he told Edwards. "This silence is ominous. I will try and see the man that you saw at the Ministry of Finance first, and ask him what is happening. But, also, I must hire a car and go and visit the fabrication works of our Venezuelan construction partner. I know that it is a long way from Caracas, but nobody from our group has been to see it. Driving seems to be the only way to get there. We do not even know that they are capable of doing the work that they say that they are going to do." The Finance Director then grinned at Edwards. "It's a hard job, but somebody has got to do it," he said.

Edwards sensed that this man had been in his office for too long. He wanted an overseas trip, for an adventure. He certainly did not want to stop him from going.

"How long will you spend there?" Edwards asked him.

"Well, I am certainly not going to go for just a few days, like you did," was the reply. "I will not rush it. I will go there for a full week, and see something of the country as well!"

4

So a few weeks later, the Finance Director left for Caracas. He, of course, had the opportunity of travelling First Class, which he took. He was away for a full week, as he said that he would be. When he came back, Edwards arranged a meeting with him to hear the result.

"Well, I spent the first few days in Caracas," the Finance Director told Edwards. "I met your "Public Schoolboy" in the Ministry of Finance. He was very charming and explained that, despite reminding the lawyer in Panama City several times, no news had yet come back from there, about this project. But he was still hopeful that they would eventually get the go-ahead and the extra finance required."

"Then I drove myself for over four hundred miles to the Orinoco," the Finance Director continued. "It took me the whole day. I met the owner of the company there, that evening. He had booked me into a grotty hotel, in the small town, by the river. The next day he showed me around his fabrication works. As I suspected, they are probably incapable of carrying out the work that they have to do for this project properly."

"So we will have to do more of the work ourselves?" asked Edwards.

"Yes," was the reply. "But, of course, that will need more money for us to do this, and the Panamanians will have to come up with even more funding."

Edwards sighed. "I cannot see the project happening now," he said.

The Finance Director paused; he seemed to have something else to tell Edwards about his visit. "I stayed another night, in the grotty hotel, that had been booked for me," the Finance Director went on. "Then, I started to drive back to Caracas. It was a lovely day, and there were some mountains in the distance. On a whim, I decided to turn off the main road and drove towards them. And then it happened!" Edwards waited, he sensed that he had to give his colleague the time to explain what seemed to have been some unfortunate incident, on his long journey.

"I soon found myself in the foothills of the mountains," continued the Finance Director. "Then I came to a small town. It was most peculiar." Edwards listened carefully, he was by now fascinated. "The buildings were all built in an Austrian style," went on the Director. "You could have easily been in the foothills of the Alps, in Germany or in Austria. There was just one main street, with a few streets going off it. It was so unusual, and somehow old-fashioned. I spotted what looked like a café or a restaurant. I decided that I needed a coffee and something to eat. I parked the car and went in."

"I used to go skiing in Austria or Switzerland, when I was younger," he explained to Edwards. "Inside, it was exactly like many of the places that I had visited, after I had been skiing, for a meal or a drink. The people there were just like those in the Alps as well: tall, white, with mainly blonde hair and blue eyes. There were four older men at a large table, in the corner. They were playing cards, and had large glasses of beer in front of them. They were dressed very formally, in old-fashioned clothes. They all turned to look at me, they seemed very suspicious of me. Then there were two middle-aged ladies, both smartly dressed in rather old-fashioned outfits. They were having coffee and cakes together at a smaller table, and seemed to be friends just meeting for a chat. They both looked me up and down. I felt embarrassed because I had left my jacket in the car, and was just in my shirt-sleeves."

"Then the young waitress came to my table from behind the small bar," he continued. "She was dressed in a dirndl, a traditional Austrian dress, and she asked me in German what I wanted! I tried English, but she could not speak it. So I asked her for a menu, in my schoolboy German, and then selected Bratwurst, Sauerkraut and a small beer. I listened to the conversation around me; it was all in German. The ladies were talking about their children; it seemed that they had to go soon and collect them from school. Then I asked for a dessert, and the waitress brought me a trolley of delicious German cakes to choose from, and a good, strong coffee, that I had also requested."

By now Edwards was fascinated, but there was more to come. "At the end of my meal, it seemed strange to have to pay for it all in Venezuelan Bolivars," continued the Finance Director. " I used the toilet, then headed back to the car. I decided to drive down one of the side streets, to see if all the houses were built in the same style. They were. The street ended in a dead end, so I turned the car around, and started to drive back to the main road. It was then that I saw it. I put my foot down on the accelerator, and got out of that town fast!"

"But what did you see?" asked Edwards, quietly.

"There was a very large stone house," replied the Finance Director. "It was set back from the road, and built like a German manor house. It must have been the largest house in the town, and I sensed that it belonged to the most important family living there. In the large, very neat, front garden, was a flagpole. At the top of that flagpole, there was a flag, fluttering in the breeze coming from the mountains. It was a red flag, with a white circle in the centre. In the white circle, was a large, black Swastika!"

Edwards gasped. "I have heard stories that some of the senior Nazis escaped from Germany, at the end of the Second World War, and went to live in South America," he said.

"I fear that I might have discovered some of them," was all that the Finance Director would say.

Edwards heard nothing back from the "Public Schoolboy" in Caracas. After his and his Director's experience in Venezuela, he decided not to contact him again. If he had have heard anything, he would only then have had to ask for even more money for his company. He told the Marketing Director of the bridge building company about what the Finance Director had discovered, on his visit to the fabrication works on the banks of the River Orinoco. He did not tell him about this man's visit to the strange German-speaking town. Fortunately, the Marketing Director agreed that it was a project no longer worth pursuing.

As far as Edwards knew, the new bridge over the River Orinoco, at that planned site, was never built. For Edwards and his colleagues, it really had proved to be "A Bridge Too Far." For Venezuela, the country's decline continued. Politicians can often do little to really change a country, be they on the right, or the left of the political spectrum. The basic nature of a country does not change; not its geographical advantages or disadvantages, its language or its culture. Unfortunately, neither does its underlying morality.

Once a Kleptocracy is established, because of human greed, it can prove very difficult to bring it to an end. Once criminals are in charge, at the top of a society, the morality of a country declines, and all kinds of other criminals are tolerated. Generations of elite leaders, of all political beliefs and skin colours, who are nothing more than corrupt thieves, can easily destroy the potential riches given by nature to any country. They can turn it into a country of poverty for their fellow citizens and, all too soon, into a country in an advanced stage of decomposition! Despite its very large oil riches, over the decades, this is what, sadly, has happened to Venezuela.

THE TIME MACHINE

We should strive to welcome change and challenges, because they are what help us grow." – H.G. Wells.

1

Edwards's work seemed to be ever expanding and this, coupled with a heavy program of overseas travel, was putting a constant strain on him and his family. It was now the second half of the 1980s. At last, he had been able to convince his Directors that he needed some more help. He had been authorised to recruit two more, qualified, senior people, for his department. He had also been told that he could expand his administrative staff, from one secretary to two, with an additional Personal Assistant for himself. But he had decided to promote his long serving and excellent secretary Liz, to be his Personal Assistant. He would then also recruit two younger secretaries for her to supervise, and to look after the needs of his two new senior team members as well.

Liz had joined him as his secretary some five years before; she had previously worked as one of the Personal Assistants to the Group Chief Executive. One day, Edwards had asked her why she had left this previous role as it seemed to offer interesting work, with good prospects for promotion? She had looked straight at him and then answered forthrightly in her Northern English accent. "You don't know what went with that job, do you? He expected all his attractive, female staff to submit to his sexual requirements! I was just not prepared to accept that."

Some years later, the Group Chief Executive would receive a Knighthood, as part of a deal with the government, where he had substantially reduced a valid claim that the Group had, in respect of a major contract in the North Sea. At least this "dishonourable honour" probably saved the British taxpayer several hundred million Pounds!

It had then taken a long time to recruit the right people that he needed. He had had to examine the details of many prospective employees that had already been screened by the employment agency, which had been used to advertise for, and initially interview, suitable candidates. After many months, he had interviewed four prospective candidates and had then decided on the two best qualified people that he wanted. They were then invited in to meet the group's Personnel Department, who would discuss their salaries and other terms of their engagement, before signing employment contracts and then working out the required notice period at their current positions.

After all these delays, his help eventually arrived. James was a Cornishman, who had worked for a Merchant Bank in the City of London. He was experienced, quick, and intelligent. With the proper briefing from Edwards, he would quickly be able to take up some of the multitude of potential overseas construction projects that Edwards had been working on. Edwards was not egotistical, and he treated his two new colleagues as equals, although he was recognised as the head of his small department. The second new addition was Caroline; she had attended one of the leading girl's private schools in the country. She was charming and well educated. Her degree was in French Language and Literature and she, of course, spoke perfect French, as well as some Spanish and Italian. She had then worked for some years for a leading international bank.

Edwards always liked and respected women in the workplace. He found that they brought a different dimension to the work and were most often more perceptive than men. Whereas a man could easily go off on some "flight of fancy", women proved to be more practical, and have their feet more firmly planted on the ground. Edwards had a trio of senior lady bankers, all of which he knew well. They had all climbed their way to the top, based upon their abilities, over the heads of their male colleagues. Whenever he had a particularly difficult problem, he would select one or two of them to consult about it, and give them a pleasant lunch in order to gain, in strict confidence, their best possible advice. That was the other good thing about women: he had found that if you made clear to them that the conversation was confidential, they did not then talk about it to others, even to their own close colleagues at their bank!

The Managing Director of one of the construction companies that Edwards looked after, asked him if he could make use of Caroline. His company had, by then, designed and built more hotels around the world, than any other building contractor. He wanted to expand this business, and to use Caroline to work closely with a former Marketing Director of that company, who had built up a lot of experience in the hotel sector. George had retired early from full-time work, some years before, because he had experienced a mild heart attack. But he still served the company as a part-time Consultant, with a specialisation in the hotel sector. Edwards agreed, rather reluctantly, to this request but, he knew that otherwise, he would still continue to be plagued by the numerous, tenuous requests from this company's Marketing Department to finance potential hotel projects, all around the world.

So many of these proposed hotel projects, were just not financeable. Although he had tried to educate these marketing staff about the basics of successful financing, time and time again, they would approach Edwards with projects that he could instantly see could just not be financed. These marketing staff seemed all too willing to jump on to an aeroplane to visit some faraway, overseas site, usually in a pleasant, warm, seaside location, where there was some would-be entrepreneur with a hotel project to construct. Only when they had returned from their overseas trip, would they then consult Edwards. In ninety per cent of the cases, Edwards could tell them straight away, that even on the basic initial information that they had, this particular new hotel project would never happen, simply because it could never be financed!

2

So it was that Caroline had "drawn the short straw." With George, she had to visit numerous, prospective hotel sites, to ascertain if this new proposed hotel could actually be financed? Edwards told her that he was sorry for her! Because of George's contacts, most of the proposed projects seem to be on beautiful, Caribbean islands, and most of their visits seemed to take place during the worst of the British winter weather. Her working relationship with George developed; in the end, he seemed to go nowhere without her. Although he had successfully transferred all her travel costs to the relevant company's Marketing

Department budget, Edwards still felt that he had to ask her some questions.

"Why does George, want you to go everywhere, with him?" he had asked her, during one of her increasingly rare visits to the office.

She thought for a moment, and then smiled at him. "I think that he is just frightened that when he goes to one of these wilder places, he may have another heart attack," she replied. "If the health service is not all that good where we are going, he wants someone with him, to look after things in case he becomes ill again."

George was much older than Caroline, but you could never tell. "I hope that your relationship, with him, is strictly professional?" enquired Edwards, with a grin on his face.

"Of course it is!" snapped back Caroline. "Do you think that I would be interested in an Old Fogey like that?" They laughed together, but then Caroline became more serious. "Just between us," she said, "I think that he has some mental problems too. Although he is old enough to be my father, sometimes I feel that I am almost a mother to him. It is the way that he confides in me, and always asks my advice, on all his personal matters."

Edwards nodded, as he had begun to understand their complex, personal relationship.

Caroline owned a small flat, just a short underground train ride from the office block, in West London, where they all worked. She had turned down the offer of a car provided by the company, which she was entitled to, and had asked for and obtained an increased salary instead. Edwards knew that she already owned a sports car, which had been a present from her parents. Unlike Edwards, who used his free company car and petrol to drive into the office, where he also had a free parking space, rather than face an expensive and unreliable train journey, she used to arrive very early into the office, every morning, when she was actually in the country.

George had once complained to Edwards that he could not sleep properly, and when he did visit the office, occasionally, he always arrived early too. Sometimes, when Edwards arrived later, he saw them together in Caroline's office, deep in conversation about their prospective hotel projects. When this happened, he always knocked on her door, and then opened it and put his head round to say a cheery "Good Morning." He would then ask them how they were getting on, and would sit down for a while to hear a short summary of the progress on the various projects that they were working on. Every month, like Edwards and James,

Caroline had to prepare a written report on each project that she was working on, and then they would, on an agreed day, all sit down to compare notes with the Group's Finance Director, to whom they all ultimately reported.

One morning, Caroline had arrived early in the office, as she usually did. After a few minutes, she was not surprised to see George enter her office. He said that he had just popped in to have a cup of coffee, and quickly exchange some news and views with her. He was on his way to Heathrow Airport, and was booked on a midday flight to New York, where he was due to stay several days, in order to visit a number of American hotel companies who had their headquarters in that city. He told her that he would be staying at the New York Plaza Hotel. They talked a little about his trip, and then about some of their proposed Caribbean projects.

Then George excused himself. "I must get off to Heathrow Airport now," he said. "I like to just sit down and relax in the Business Class Lounge, and read the papers they provide there before boarding the aircraft." Caroline wished him a safe flight and a successful trip, and then he left.

3

What happened next, would be the subject of a true story that Edwards would tell for many years afterwards. By the time that Edwards had arrived in the office, that morning, Caroline had already left. He would not hear what had actually happened, until she had returned, some two days later. A few minutes after George had left her office, Caroline's telephone had rung. She picked it up; it was the Main Board Director, whom they all detested. He was an egotistical, bumptious individual, who never listened to anyone else's opinion. But towards Caroline, he was always polite and charming.

Caroline suspected that he had some, as yet, undeclared, interest in her. Although he was a married man, his wife and children lived most of the time up in Yorkshire, while he occupied their London flat. Caroline somehow expected, at some future date, to receive an invitation to an expensive dinner and then a request that she might become his mistress? But she was determined that she would have absolutely nothing to do with that role, even if it might be detrimental to her future career at the Group!

"I want you to go to New York for me," he told her, in his gruff Northern accent. "There is a very senior banker there that has invited me to dinner, and now I have a very important appointment here, and I cannot go. I think that you will deputise for me very well."

"Of course," said Caroline helpfully. "When do you want me to go there?"

"The dinner is tonight!" was the reply.

Caroline nearly dropped the telephone. "But how do you expect me to get there in time?" she asked sensibly.

"That's no problem," was the instant reply. "You can take this afternoon's Concorde flight. I will authorise your flight, now, with our Travel Agency, and you can pick up your ticket at the airport. To save some money, you can come back tomorrow by an ordinary flight. I will ask them to also issue you with a return ticket. First class, naturally!"

He then provided Caroline with the banker's name, the time set for the dinner, and the name and address of the expensive Manhattan restaurant where he and the banker had been due to meet that evening.

"Don't worry," he said. "I will telephone him as soon as he is in his office, and tell him that I cannot make it. But I am sending you instead on Concorde, and tell him what a wonderful girl you are!"

Caroline left the office, immediately, and hurried back to her flat. She packed an overnight carry-on bag, grabbed her Passport, and called for a taxi to take her to Heathrow Airport. At the Airport, she collected her two air tickets from the British Airways desk, and then checked in at the special Concorde section, at the end of the Departures terminal. She was soon through the dedicated Concorde fast-track Security Channel, and then into the luxury Concorde Lounge, to wait for her flight. She was both agitated and excited, and needed a couple of glasses of the best Champagne that was, of course, free and available in the Lounge, just to steady her nerves!

4

Soon she was on the aircraft; it seemed a very narrow fuselage, compared with the other aeroplanes that she usually flew on. But her seat was luxurious, and very comfortable. Concorde had priority over other aircraft, and very soon it took off with a great roar of its four Rolls Royce Olympus turbo jet engines, each fitted with an afterburner, to greatly increase its power.

Although it took just over a hundred passengers, they travelled in absolute first class comfort, and paid a lot of money for that privilege, and the time that they saved in travelling. Soon, Caroline was eleven miles up, over the Atlantic Ocean, and flying at twice the speed of sound. This was more than twice the speed of any conventional aircraft.

Then a delicious meal, accompanied by the best wines available, was served to her. Only then, did she seem to have the time to think. Where would she spend the night? Then she remembered that George had told her, early that morning, that he would be staying at the New York Plaza Hotel. That would be as good a place as any to sleep that night. Concorde was a virtual "Time Machine". It took only three and a half hours to cross between London and New York. You arrived at New York one and a half hours earlier, in local time, than the local time when you had left London.

When they arrived at John F. Kennedy Airport, again Concorde had priority. The fast-track Concorde Immigration line, and the fact that she only had hand-luggage, meant that she was out of the airport terminal quickly, and into a New York Yellow Cab, bound for the Plaza Hotel. It was now past the local lunch break, and the traffic was light. She arrived at the New York Plaza Hotel, and went straight to Reception. Fortunately, they had an

Executive Room to offer her for the night. Just at that moment, George passed through the main entrance doors, followed by the hotel porter carrying his case, and also made his way towards the Reception desk to check-in, and claim his own room.

Suddenly, he saw Caroline and his mouth dropped open! The briefcase he was carrying fell to the marble floor of the hotel lobby, from his lifeless grasp, with a loud crash. George could not believe his eyes; he had left Caroline twelve hours ago, in her London office, and here she was, checking in, in front of him, in his New York hotel! The colour drained from his face, and he staggered backwards in shock. He looked as if he was about to faint. Caroline saw him, and realised what was happening, she really feared that he might have another heart attack on the spot! She ran to him, to tell him the story of what had happened since he had left her, only that morning, all the way back in London.

After her hurried explanation, as he was obviously still in a state of shock, Caroline helped George check in at the Reception Desk. Then she got the porter to take his case and show him up to his room. As soon as the pair had entered the elevator and its doors had closed, Caroline took another elevator up to her floor to find her own Executive Room. It was very comfortable, but she now felt tired, probably from all the excitement of the day so far. She closed the curtains, undressed, and got into bed. She was very aware of what "jet lag" could do to you and she wanted to be in "top form" for her dinner that evening.

The combination of the fine Concorde food, the wines, and the Champagne, ensured that she slept for over two hours. She got up, ran herself a hot bath, and luxuriated in it for another half-hour. Then she washed her hair, dried it, and coiffured it carefully. She applied her best make-up, which she had brought with her, before getting dressed into the smart but attractive, and rather revealing outfit that she had quickly selected to wear back in her London flat.

She was now looking forward to what, she was sure, would be an excellent dinner, and to meeting the very senior New York banker, who was to be her host for the evening. To complete her preparations, she added several, large dabs of her favourite perfume, to the appropriate places. She hoped that, after all this frantic, unexpected travelling, her dinner companion, even if he was not handsome, would turn out to be, at least, in some ways, sophisticated and charming!

HOT LIPS

"When I went to Hong Kong, I knew at once I wanted to write a story set there." – Paul Theroux.

1

There was a great crash, as the Chinese waiter accidently dropped the large silver tray that he was carrying. It bounced twice then rolled on its rim for at least five yards, before finally falling on its face, with a further loud rattle. Edwards was just as startled as the other guests having breakfast in the opulent hotel dining room. The Head Waiter hurried forward to admonish his very embarrassed underling, and to publically apologise to the guests for the shock that they had suffered. Edwards recovered quickly and started again to eat his excellent full English Breakfast, which had been brought to his table, and served by another of the waiters with great panache. He smiled to himself as he thought that the service in this hotel was so perfect, that it needed something like this to happen, to remind you that, even here, things can go wrong too!

Edwards was staying in the Mandarin Oriental Hotel, on Hong Kong Island. It was probably one of the most luxurious hotels in the World. He had been staying there now for over a week, and he was beginning to get a little bored of the perfect cocoon, in which he lived. Hong Kong was a vibrant and interesting place but, at times, felt a little claustrophobic. Despite being only some thirty miles from mainland China, this British Colony seemed to live as if it was totally separated, by thousands of miles, from the over one billion people of the Communist People's Republic of China, just up the road. It was now 1986; it would not be until July 1997, that Hong Kong would be handed back to China by Britain. Meanwhile it remained a strange anachronism, still governed under British Colonial rule.

On an earlier trip to Hong Kong, Edwards had visited the "Noble House", as it was called in this British Colony. This was the trading house of Jardine Matheson, which had been closely tied up with the history of Hong Kong. This firm had been founded in Canton in 1832, by two Scotsmen, William Jardine and James Matheson. However, the firm had moved to Hong Kong in 1842, when the British had been ceded Hong Kong Island by the Treaty of Nanking, following the defeat of China, in what became known as the First Opium War. The two founders had already made a fortune out of the trading of tea, other commodities, and opium into China. It was the trade in opium, which was destroying the health of a large part of the Chinese population, which had caused a series of wars with the British.

When the Chinese government had refused to import any more opium, and had destroyed all the existing stocks, the British claimed that this was an affront to their "Free Trade Policy", and declared war on China. The antiquated Chinese navy had been completely destroyed by a small number of British naval vessels. As a result of this First Opium War, the British gained Hong Kong Island and some of the surrounding islands, granted to them in perpetuity. They later added Kowloon on the opposite mainland, on a 99 year lease basis, following the Second Opium War. The British then leased more land, north of Kowloon, from a now compliant Chinese government, which became known as the New Territories.

Edwards had once purchased a book at Singapore Airport; it was called "Foreign Mud", which was the name the Chinese had given the opium that they had been forced to continue importing. It had been written by an American academic who had been asked to write the official history of Jardine Matheson. Instead he had written a true history of how this illustrious company had made a fortune as a result of being very successful drug dealers. The "Noble House" was appalled by this, their true history, and tried to ban publication of the book. But the author had still managed to get it published. Needless to say, the book remained banned in Hong Kong.

One of the directors of the construction group that Edwards now worked for, had suggested that he should meet one of the senior management members of the "Noble House". Edwards's director was a pompous man, strongly disliked by all the people that had to work with him. He already knew this man in Hong Kong, and had suggested that Edwards should brief him about the work that he was doing there. So, one morning, Edwards had taken a taxi from his hotel to the tall building on the edge of Hong Kong Island, which looked over the great harbour. The name Hong Kong, in the local Cantonese language, meant "Fragrant Harbour", although, with the vast amount of shipping now using it, it was no longer very fragrant! The harbour had, of course, been renamed Victoria Harbour by the British, in honour of their then Queen.

Edwards well remembered his visit to Jardine Matheson. He was to meet one of its directors, whose name betrayed that he was also the head of a Scottish Clan. He was shown into a special lift, which would take him up to the top Executive Floor. A Receptionist then took him down a long corridor, whose walls were covered with ancient Chinese paintings. He was shown into an outer office, where he met the man's Secretary. Finally, when the director was ready to receive him, she opened the great double doors to his inner office. It was huge, richly furnished and ornately decorated. At the far end, the "Great Man" was sitting behind an enormous desk. As he advanced across the room, the rich pile of the carpet seemed to get thicker and thicker. Edwards really had to struggle, to make the last thirty feet of his long walk!

He was met with a rather grudging handshake and a complete disinterest in what he had to say. Who was this lower-class interloper, who wanted to take some precious minutes of the "Great Man's" day? The Jardine Matheson building is unusual in having large, circular windows, like ship's portholes. The Hong Kong Chinese had a nickname for it; translating from the local Cantonese language, it was known as "The Building of the Thousand Cunts." Edwards could never quite work out whether this local Chinese name referred to its round windows, or to the people who actually worked inside the building!

2

Edwards's arrival in Hong Kong, this time, had been just as exciting as his previous arrivals. He had enjoyed the very comfortable business class service of a Cathay Pacific flight from London. He had then experienced the usual, hair-raising landing at the, then, Hong Kong Airport of Kai Tak. The landing there was perhaps one of the most difficult in the world, and most Airline Captains saw it as a real challenge. Sometimes, as they began their descent, they would try to frighten their passengers by announcing on the public address system, that they were handing the landing over to their Co-Pilot, just to give them the experience!

Each aeroplane had to carefully weave its way through the rugged high hills surrounding Kowloon, and then through a series of skyscrapers, turning first left, and then right, with a final very rapid descent onto the runway, which jutted out into Hong Kong harbour. Take offs were just as exciting too; because of the short runway, the pilot had to apply maximum power before the aircraft even began to move, and once the brakes were released, the aircraft shot forward. But some did not make it, and during one of Edwards's previous visits, a Lufthansa aircraft failed to take off in time, and nearly ended up in the Harbour. The pilot aborted the take off just in time, but the aircraft was badly damaged. Fortunately, this time, there was no loss of life.

By now, Edwards quite enjoyed this spectacular landing. He watched from his window seat and tried to judge the expertise of the pilot, as he flew the large aircraft just the right distance from each of the surrounding skyscrapers. But Edwards was quietly looking out for just one particular building, which always amused him. It was a high glass tower, occupied by a Chinese company. At its top was the company's name in large, red, illuminated, capital letters. The name simply read "FUKU"!

Edwards's full English Breakfast that morning, he thought, was supposed to be some kind of antidote to the large amount of alcohol that he had drunk the night before. The same pompous director, who had asked him to visit the "Noble House", had asked him to meet the joint owners of a British engineering consulting company that he knew, and who were staying in the same hotel as Edwards. Edwards had called one of them on the hotel's internal telephone, earlier in the day, and he had asked Edwards to join him for dinner that evening. The dinner was held in the top floor restaurant of the hotel, with its stunning nighttime views over the twinkling lights of Hong Kong harbour.

This was probably the most expensive restaurant in Hong Kong, and they were given a table by the window. His host seemed to want to impress him by spending lavishly from his expenses budget. The man was joined by his business partner, who owned the rest of the company and both their wives. The ladies were beautifully dressed, and sparkled with large amounts of expensive jewellery. The meal commenced with several bottles of the most expensive Champagne, and the first course was, of course, Beluga Caviar. This was followed by an expensive fish dish, and then the best steaks available. The food was accompanied with copious amounts of the finest white and red French wines. Afterwards, the required expensive dessert, coffee, digestives, and cigars were served.

It was only after the ladies had retired to bed, that the serious drinking started, and the two men had begun to question Edwards about his business activities. They had both now turned to drinking beer, but Edwards, he thought wisely, had stayed with the red wine. The result had been a largely sleepless night and a pounding headache in the morning! But he did wonder how the heads of his two drinking companions from the night before, must have felt? He did notice that there was no sign of either of them, or their wives, at breakfast that following morning.

His appointment that morning was with one of the Partners in a leading Hong Kong firm of Estate Agents. Their offices were over in Kowloon, and he had been asked to visit them to gain their views on the future of the Hong Kong property market, and on one particular large residential project, which one of the construction companies that he looked after had an interest in. Rather than take a taxi through the tunnel under the harbour, Edwards walked down to the terminal and took the ferry to Kowloon, to clear his head. The views over Hong Kong harbour, were as splendid as usual, and the sea air helped his nagging headache to disappear.

Edwards always said, to those that would listen, that there were only two cities in the world, where you could believe that everything was possible. One of them was New York, and the other was Hong Kong. Maybe it was the effect of the high buildings, but Edwards always sensed a strange tingle of electricity in the air, of both cities. In both cities too, there was a free, or a very cheap ferry ride that was worth taking. In New York, it was the Staten Island Ferry, and in Hong Kong, it was the Star Ferry, which crossed Victoria Harbour between the main island of Hong Kong and Kowloon on the mainland. Both ferry rides gave you a spectacular view, from the water, of the city.

From the ferry terminal on "Kowloon Side", Edwards took a taxi to the offices of the Estate Agents, which were housed in one of the numerous, new office blocks, that now covered the shoreline of both Hong Kong island and Kowloon. Further back, were the innumerable massive blocks of flats that were occupied by the Chinese workers and their families, who provided all of the real work force of this British Colony. He was received by the firm's Partner, in their luxurious offices, on the tenth floor of the building. He was an Australian in his mid-thirties, and exhibited the somewhat rough charm of his countrymen.

Edwards liked the Australians; unlike many English people they had no pretence about themselves, and always worked very hard, and played hard as well. He received a first-class summary of the current state of the local property market, and its probable future. The two men then started to discuss the project that

Edwards's company had in mind. The Australian showed his knowledge of the location for the development, by suggesting several improvements that could be made in their plans. Edwards was impressed; his suggestions were all very practical and would not cost very much to do. But, they would probably increase the selling prices for the development considerably.

After they had finished their discussion, he looked at Edwards: "How long are you staying?" he asked. Edwards told him that he intended to be in Hong Kong until a week the following Saturday, when he was due to fly back to London on the evening flight. "Come out with me on that Friday night, before you go back. We can have some dinner together. Then, I will show you some of the night life. I have been here now for over five years, so I should know my way around," said the Australian.

Edwards willingly agreed and then, as an afterthought asked "Would your wife like to come too?"

The Australian laughed. "I am not married," he said. "At least, not permanently. There are so many attractive Chinese women around here that want to be with Europeans, that marriage is really not a requirement!"

3

The following morning, Edwards was due to meet the local Project Manager of one of the companies that he looked after. They were involved in building the huge steel skeleton of a new major building, for an international bank, on Hong Kong Island. He took a taxi to the nearby site, and was met by the Manager at its entrance.

"Let's go for a cup of coffee," he said, and led Edwards to a nearby building. They took the lift to the twelfth floor. "There is a decent restaurant here," said the Project Manager. "But, this time of the day, they do an excellent coffee." They sat down, at a window table, looking over the building site next door.

"This is where I come so I can watch progress on my site, in comfort," the man said. Edwards looked out of the window, and he was horrified! The local Chinese workmen were scampering freely along the steel girder structure that had so far been completed, and against which had been placed a frail, rickety-looking, bamboo scaffolding. He remarked to his colleague about it.

"They are ok," he replied. "They are used to such building methods, and prepared to take such risks." Edwards concluded that, in South East Asia, like in Africa where he had also travelled, the price of Human Life was considered to be very cheap!

"Why I wanted to talk to you," continued the Project Manager, "is that we need some more money. You will remember that you set up an Export Credit loan supported by the British Government, to cover the cost of the steel that we are importing from the U.K., and also for all our work here. Now we will need to import a lot more steel, and there will be the extra costs, here, of putting it into the steel structure."

"But why do you need more?" asked Edwards.

The Project Manager smiled at him. "Well," he said "we had the benefit, on this job, of having a Creative Architect! He designed this building with too little steel. As we have been building it up, we have found that the stresses and strains in the building, are just too much. We have now had to redesign it, and have had to double the amount of steel needed. Otherwise, it could just fall down."

Edwards gasped. "Well alright then," he replied. "Just let me have the figures and the agreement, of course, of the bank who are guaranteeing the loan, and I will see what I can do. I cannot see any reason that, in principal, the amount of the loan cannot be increased, to provide finance for the extra steel and for all the additional work needed." He smiled at his colleague, "It is all good business for you," he added.

This meeting over, Edwards quickly took a taxi to his temporary office. He had an urgent duty to perform. It had been arranged that he would be on an exchange visit for three weeks, with a medium-sized construction company in Hong Kong. His construction group used this local company as a sub-contractor, to provide vital local services and labour for the various projects that they were undertaking in Hong Kong. The Finance Director of this company had gone to London for the same three weeks, to learn more about Edwards's group of companies, and Edwards had come here. The local company had offices on several floors of a high-rise building on Hong Kong Island, and Edwards had been given the Finance Director's office to work from. It was much larger than his office back in London, and contained a large, illuminated fish tank, full of highly coloured, tropical fish. Apparently, keeping tropical fish was the hobby of the Finance Director, who had a Scottish surname.

The first morning, when Edwards had arrived on his temporary assignment, the Finance Director had politely stayed back, in Hong Kong, for the day, in order to receive him. He said that he wanted to introduce him to his fellow Directors. But maybe he had an ulterior motive, as some of his first words were "Please feed the fish, when you arrive, and when you leave the office, every day." He then handed Edwards a large container of fish food.

"But how much?" asked Edwards.

"Here, let me show you," said the Finance Director, taking back the container and sprinkling some food into the tank. The voracious fish rose immediately to the top of the tank to eat. "They will be alright for the three weeks that I will be away. The lights work on a timer, and the tank keeps the water clean automatically," he added.

He had then taken Edwards to meet his Managing Director; he was a cultivated and affable man. He was, like the Finance Director and all the other Directors that Edwards was then introduced to, either Scottish or English, but all were permanent residents of Hong Kong. Most of the rest of the staff were Chinese, and Edwards was then introduced to the pretty, but very efficient, Chinese girl, who would act as his secretary during his stay.

"I must mention that every Wednesday morning, we have a Board Meeting, and while you are here, you are invited to attend," said the Finance Director, as he walked Edwards down the long corridor, between various offices. "This Wednesday, the Board has asked that after the Board Meeting, you might give them a Presentation on what you do in London, and educate them a little please, on the world of High Finance!" He grinned at Edwards. "Sorry to put you right in it," he said. "But I am sure that you are capable of quickly putting something together to say to them."

He suddenly remembered something else, and took a key out of his pocket. "I nearly forgot," he said. "Here is a spare key to the Executive Toilets. Please leave it with your Secretary when you go back to London."

Edwards was amused. "Don't we use the same facilities as the staff?" he asked.

"Oh no, that would never do!" had been the curt reply.

After he had fed the fish that morning, Edwards had one more urgent task to complete. Every night, the Chinese office cleaner, who cleaned his office, would move every picture on the walls of the office, out of the strictly perpendicular. The local Chinese considered that it was "Bad Joss", or bad luck, for anything to be absolutely straight. So Edwards took a delight, every morning, in moving back every picture to its proper position. He actually found it very disconcerting to sit behind the desk, and see things that were not correctly aligned!

The first weekend of his stay, the Managing Director had invited him to come to his home, for Sunday Lunch. He lived on the southern shore of Hong Kong Island at Repulse Bay which, after The Peak, where the British Governor lived, was probably the most expensive residential area on the island. "My wife is back in England, visiting relatives," he had said. "But I will cook lunch for us." So, at midday on Sunday, Edwards had taken a taxi from his hotel, across the island, to Repulse Bay. The ride should have taken only twenty minutes, but the taxi driver seemed to take him on a circular route, up and down the hills in the centre of the island, giving Edwards a good view of the Happy Valley horseracing course, on the way.

When they arrived at Repulse Bay, the driver then had to find the right block of luxury flats, in which the Managing Director lived. At last, they found the right block, and Edwards found the right flat within it. He was welcomed inside. It had a large living and dining area, with a spacious balcony, overlooking the South China Sea. As soon as it was polite to do so, Edwards asked to use the lavatory, which he needed after the long taxi ride. He was shown, by his host, to a small toilet, off the hallway. After an aperitif, the Managing Director produced the first course: it was a steaming bowl of soup.

"This is one of my specialities," he said. "It is based on a Thai recipe. I hope that you will not find it too hot." Edwards tried it. It exploded in his mouth! It seemed to be crammed full of very hot spices. For Edwards, it was completely inedible!

"It is hot, but I will drink it slowly," he said, smiling at his host. The other man quickly finished his soup, with relish. He then apologised, and disappeared into the kitchen, to prepare the next course. After just a few moments, Edwards had to use the lavatory again. But, this time, unbeknown to his host, he took the soup bowl with him. He rapidly, but carefully, emptied it down the lavatory, and then flushed the soup away. By the time that his host brought in the second course of the Sunday lunch, Edwards was sitting back again, on his seat at the table, with his empty soup bowl set proudly in front of him!

4

Quickly, his last evening in Hong Kong, had come around. He had the promised invitation from the Australian Estate Agent, to fulfil. He was looking forward to being shown a little of the night life of Hong Kong, by a person who was an obvious expert. He waited in the Hotel Reception, at the agreed time. Soon the Australian breezed in and waved at him. "I have got my car outside," he said. Edwards followed him and was led to a blood-red, very expensive, Porsche sports car. Edwards though that this was a little superfluous because the road system in Hong Kong, combined with the small size of the Colony and the large amount of traffic, meant that cars were hardly ever able to drive at more than a maximum of thirty to forty miles an hour.

Edwards struggled to get into the low, front, passenger seat of the luxury sports car. "I know a good, but inexpensive, Chinese restaurant in Wan Chai," said the Australian. "Let's go there first, for a quick dinner, then we can hit the town." He accelerated hard, away from the hotel, and they were soon in the Wan Chai district on Hong Kong Island.

Edwards remembered seeing Wan Chai, photographed, years ago, in the 1960 film "The World of Suzie Wong", when it had been a poor area, known for its bars, its crowds of visiting sailors, and its prostitution. But it had changed out of all recognition; there was now a busy commercial centre, and numerous high-rise apartment blocks, containing thousands of the small flats that the low-paid Chinese workers inhabited.

HOT LIPS

The Australian parked his expensive car very carefully, and then it was only a short walk to his chosen restaurant. To Edwards, it seemed a little basic, and he was always a little suspicious about Chinese food, but the Australian reassured him.

"I have eaten here many times," he said. "The food is very good, and I have never had any stomach problems afterwards." Their dinner completed, they returned to the Porsche.

"Now for the Bottoms Up," said the Australian, driving them through the Cross Harbour Tunnel, under Victoria Harbour, to Kowloon.

Despite his previous visits, Edwards had not been to the famous "Bottoms Up Club." Soon, the Australian was again parking his car. They walked to the narrow entrance of the Club, with its sign of a pair of naked female buttocks. Inside, they sat at the bar and were served by a beautiful, topless Chinese waitress, who sat on top of the broad, bar counter, so that the customers could get a full view of her.

The bar was packed with visitors from all over the world. Then, the topless troupe of dancers appeared on a raised dais and performed their music and dance act. The Australian stifled a yawn, "This is not as good as Hot Lips," he said. "I will take you there after we have made visits to a few more places. Hot Lips is quite the hottest place in town!"

After over an hour at the Bottoms Up, they decided to leave. They had now seen the dancers performing their act twice over. "We can walk to the next place," said Edwards's companion. He took them down an alleyway, and into a much smaller bar. Again, they sat at the bar and watched a number of strip-tease acts, accompanied by recorded music, given by a series of beautiful, young Chinese girls.

"They are not as beautiful as the girls at Hot Lips," said the Australian. "You wait until you see them!" After an hour, the Australian had got bored again. "Let's go to the next place," he said.

He led Edwards back, up the alleyway, and along the main road. This time they entered a much bigger, and more expensive establishment. There was a bar with high stools, but there were also a large number of tables. They were shown to one of the tables. Edwards's companion seem to have a bottomless expenses account; he immediately ordered a bottle of Champagne, and four glasses. Soon they were joined by two beautiful Chinese girls, in dresses which left little to the imagination. Strangely, they both seemed to know the Australian already, and called him by his first name. Edwards asked him about this.

"Yes, I am a fairly regular visitor here," he replied. "If you want to take one of the girls away, to a nearby hotel, then you have to make a payment to this place, and to the girl of course!" He smiled at Edwards. "It is a bit upmarket here, but not as good as Hot Lips!"

The two Chinese girls were charming, they spoke excellent English, and were well educated. They both gave the story that they were actually university students, who were only here to pay their way through college. After a while, one of the Chinese girls began to drape herself around the Australian, while Edwards talked to the other one. The Champagne finished, the Australian, suddenly, stood up.

"Now is the time to go to Hot Lips!" he announced. Edwards looked at his watch, it was already past two o'clock in the morning. They walked back to the car. "You are in for a real treat, now," said the Australian. "Those other places have nothing on Hot Lips." He seemed to Edwards to only drive them around, in a circle, and then parked again. "Follow me," said the Australian, as they got out of the car. He grinned at Edwards, in obvious anticipation.

Edwards followed his companion for the evening, down an alleyway, off the main road. Then they turned right, down a narrower alley, and then, finally, left into an alleyway so narrow, that only one person at a time could go down it. At the end of the narrow alley was a flashing red sign. It showed a pair of lips, and underneath the words, in capital letters, "HOT LIPS". There was no door, only a curtain, which the Australian held aside for Edwards to enter.

Inside, there was one small room, with some cheap tables and chairs. At the end of the room, was a small bar. It was dark and dingy. In the dim light, Edwards began to be able to see the occupants. They were all Chinese women, but, he estimated, that none of them were under the age of fifty! They were all well made-up, and well coiffured. They were all well-dressed, but, again, in dresses which left very little to the imagination, with low bosoms and long slits up to their thighs. He reeled back and the Australian caught him, so that he would not fall!

He laughed at Edwards. "Don't worry," he said to Edwards. "They won't bite. They are all retired, or semi-retired prostitutes, who still like to keep their hand in at entertaining men. You have heard about the well-educated, Japanese Geishas? Well these are Hong Kong Geishas. They are all very experienced, have met a lot of people, know a lot about the world, and love just to talk to you."

Edwards began slowly to recover, and they both sat down at one of the small tables. The Australian grinned at him, he had played the game of higher and higher anticipation on Edwards, so well. "Mind you," he said, "If they like you, they might invite you upstairs, where there are some bedrooms. That is where some of them live. But, of course, you don't have to go up." he added.

The barmaid came around the bar, to take their orders. They were soon joined by two of the Chinese ladies, and the Australian, gallantly, ordered the expensive drinks that they wanted, for them. The two ladies soon both proved as wise and as entertaining, as Edwards's companion for the evening, had promised. Edwards relaxed; he had, at last, finally entered "The World of, the now aged, Suzy Wong!"

THE KING OF ITALY

"It is good to trust others but, not to do so, is much better" – Benito Mussolini.

1

"If Italy was not a Republic, I would now be the King of Italy!"

Edwards looked quizzically, over the top of his glasses, at his companion. They had just entered the Bar of Edwards's London Club close to Whitehall. It was a really magnificent building, built in the 1870s as a gentleman's club, but now ladies were also admitted as members. It had a number of function rooms, which were sometimes hired out to outside organisations for their events, a large Sitting Room where Edwards held many of his business meetings, a Bar, and a very pleasant Dining Room which served plain English food.

Edwards was a little taken aback by his companion's remark, but he seemed to have said it in all seriousness. He thought quickly. "But what would Your Majesty like to drink?" he asked. His companion did not seem to see his sense of humour. He went on to explain that as he was a descendant of the famous Borgias, through his mother's family, he calculated that he had a valid claim upon the Italian Throne. Edwards chose to ignore this remark and asked him again what he would like to drink.

Edwards had been introduced to this man, Peter, several years before, by his long-standing barrister friend, Brian. Peter was originally from Malta but had obtained his degrees from London University where, finally, he had received a Doctorate in International Tax Planning. He had returned to Malta and set up his own professional tax advice practice. He had also been called upon to advise one of the Maltese Governments on structuring the future tax regulations of the Maltese islands. But such was the belligerent state between the main Maltese political parties that, when the opposition won the next election and formed a new government, he was arrested on trumped-up charges and had spent some twelve months in jail, before he was finally released. He had then left Malta and gone to live in Italy, where his mother had been born. He was tall and always immaculately well dressed, with the dark and striking good looks, perhaps of the Italian nobility, which he claimed to be descended from.

Edwards knew that Peter was still active in business, and that he travelled regularly between Malta, Italy, and the United Kingdom. He had also recently spent a great deal of time in Brazil, where he claimed to have many senior contacts. He was now living back on Malta and was married with a young son, who he was very proud of. He had taught his son sailing and kept a yacht moored in Saint Julian's Harbour, one of the bays not far from the island's capital of Valletta. The young boy had grown into a teenager and was now an accomplished sailor, capable of sailing alone on the sometimes difficult seas around the Maltese islands. However, Peter's marriage had turned sour, and he now had a regular English girlfriend. He explained to Edwards that, as it was a deeply Catholic island, divorce was not yet legal on Malta. But that he hoped that the law would be changed in a few years' time, and then he would be able to seek a divorce.

"I have a possible consultancy contract to offer you, if you are interested," Peter suddenly said.

"Tell me about it," replied Edwards, who despite having now reached the normal retirement age, was still employed on a part-time basis, as an adviser to a former Government owned organisation dealing with advanced technologies. That left him free to do other things and earn some more money if he wished.

"I am working with an Italian company in Ravenna," replied Peter. "They have developed advanced technology for working with underwater pipelines and cables which need repairing or need to be buried under the seabed," he went on.

Edwards thought back to his enjoyable visits to Italy, when he had worked in the City of London, many years before. How he had met and had so innocently worked with Roberto Calvi in his dealings to export vast sums of money out of Italy. Calvi had become known as "God's Banker," as he had handled and invested large sums for the Vatican Bank and it was rumoured, for the Italian Mafia. He was found hanging by the neck in London, under Blackfriars Bridge, in June, 1982. For years the City of London Police had insisted that his death was a suicide, until it was incontrovertibly proved to them, at last, that this Italian banker had been murdered.

2

Ravenna is an ancient city, situated very close to the northern Adriatic coast of Italy. For a few years, it was the capital city of the Western Roman Empire, until this Empire collapsed in 476 CE. It then served as the capital of the invading Ostrogoths, until it was recaptured by the Byzantine Eastern Roman Empire in 540 CE. In 751 CE it was captured by the Italian Lombards, becoming the capital of their Kingdom. Ravenna is famed for its many early Christian mosaics, which remain in a pristine condition. Although he would have loved to have had some opportunity to see these, Edwards had no time to spare. Peter had collected him from Bologna Airport, after his budget flight from London. As Peter had guided his hired car around a roundabout, Edwards had caught a glimpse of the sixth century Basilica of San Vitale and, instinctively knew, what ancient treasures lay inside.

Peter drove on to the cheap hotel where they were both staying. It was only when they went out to dinner in the evening, that Edwards was able to get any real sense of the city. They walked down narrow streets to a great square, where Peter knew that they would be able to select a restaurant. It was still warm, so they sat outside, and Edwards was able to see, in the gathering twilight, the great Medieval buildings around him. From their style, he thought that they had probably been built when the Venetians had occupied the city in the fifteenth century.

Over dinner, they reviewed their strategy for the following day, when they were due to meet the Italian company. Peter explained that the company was owned and run by a husband-and-wife team. The husband was the technical genius, who had invented the sub-surface machines which carried out the underwater work. But he was hopeless as far as commercial matters were concerned. Fortunately, his wife had a good commercial sense and ran the company well. Peter had been asked by them to find some new markets for their expertise, and he had done this during his several trips to Brazil. He had made several senior contacts there with the Brazilian national oil company Petróleo Brasileiro, more commonly known as Petrobras.

But this would require an expansion in the Italian company and additional bank finance would be needed to do this. How much, for what, how it would be repaid, and where to find it, would be Edwards's job. He had to find out all the answers to any questions that he had, during this visit. Edwards felt that he could competently carry out this task; he now had years of experience in finding money for major projects, and for the sale of equipment which was to be exported from Britain. He should be able to use these same skills, to help find this Italian company the extra finance that it now needed, in order to expand.

The following morning, it was an easy walk from their hotel to the offices of the Italian company. Peter wanted them to arrive early, as he had set up some early meetings with the company's owners. That would then give Edwards the whole of the rest of the day, to start on the task in hand.

"But first, if they want me to work for them, I will need to negotiate the terms of my own consultancy contract," Edwards told Peter as they walked. Peter agreed but said that Edwards should keep any up-front payments relatively small, and then rely on a large success payment to himself, to come out of the new funding that he had identified and raised for the company, as his main reward.

They first met the owners; the husband was tall and thin. Although he only spoke Italian, which Peter translated, it was soon clear to Edwards that, like many highly-gifted technical people, he lived on "another planet!" He showed them some of the machines that he had invented and then made. They were contained in a long, low shed at the back of the company offices. He tried to explain how they, and the other underwater machines in his technical portfolio, worked. His enthusiasm for his subject was boundless! When they met his wife, Edwards found that she was different; shorter and somewhat overweight, she had a large, rather beautiful face, with sparkling eyes. She spoke good English and obviously knew very well how to run the business. It was with her that Edwards had his discussion about the terms of his appointment, while Peter went to speak to some of their marketing staff. It was finally agreed that he would receive four monthly retainer payments while he did his work, and then an attractive Success Fee, once the extra funding that they needed was made available and drawn down.

The rest of Edwards's day was spent with the company accountant, another lady with good English, and highly efficient. She provided him with all the information and the accounting details that he would need. In the evening, Peter and he had dinner together again.

"It is going well," Edwards told him. "But it will take at least another half-day of work, to get the rest of the information that I will need. Plus, I need to know what the new business opportunities are, to work out how much extra working capital they will need."

"I can give you that," said Peter quickly. "After all, I have developed all their new potential business for them. Their existing marketing people are useless. My deal will be to become their permanent Marketing Director, once I bring the new business in."

"Are you being paid already?" asked Edwards out of interest.

"Of course," replied Peter. "They have paid for all my travel expenses, Business Class of course, all my hotels, and any other expenses. Plus, they have paid me for my time."

By lunchtime the following day, Edwards was satisfied that he had received all the information that he needed. In the afternoon they were taken to the port area near Ravenna and shown, by the proud husband, a specialist vessel which the company owned.

On its deck, was another of the clever, underwater machines that he had designed, and then had engineered and assembled.

3

The following morning Peter drove Edwards back to Bologna Airport, for his return flight to London. But Edwards's work had only just begun; he now had to write a long Information Memorandum that could be presented to a possible lending bank, and would be sufficient to persuade them to lend the amount required by the Italian company. There were many days of work in front of the computer. First, Edwards had to do his own Market Analysis to convince the bank that the business in this highly specialised market sector, was actually there. Then the background to, and the current financial situation of the company, had to be presented. Finally, through carefully worked out Financial Projections, what income and profits could be achieved from any new business. Many conservative assumptions had to be made and each assumption had to be carefully explained in the document.

Of course, Edwards found he had more questions and he had to telephone or email the company accountant in Ravenna for answers. Only when he was fully satisfied with his final draft of the long document and the attached Financial Projections, was he confident enough to send it to the wife, who ran the company, for her approval. Once that had come, he could then start talking to potential bank lenders. He talked to many but, in the end, only three banks seemed interested in perhaps looking seriously at this highly specialised lending opportunity.

His first monthly retainer had been received, and his second monthly payment was now overdue. Edwards contacted the company accountant, but he was told that the matter was being handled by the wife, who part-owned and ran the business with her husband. At last, one morning, he managed to speak to her.

"I am sorry," she said in her good English. "I have decided to tell Peter that I no longer want him to represent our company. Unfortunately, you are connected with him and I cannot make any more payments under your arrangement with us."

"But we have a contract," spluttered Edwards, completely shocked by what he was being told.

"Yes," she admitted. "But your friend Peter has misled me. He claimed that he had all this new work for us in Brazil. I have now been in touch with some of the people there, directly, who do not seem to be interested in our company. I just do not believe him anymore!"

Edwards was horrified; all his efforts would be wasted and he would be embarrassed to speak to the banks that he had selected, in order to tell them that this potential business was now no longer available. It was pointless trying to sue the company for the rest of the money they owed him, as it would have to take place in an Italian Court, with all the trouble and expense of having to visit there, in order to mount a proper legal case.

For nearly a year there was no news of Peter, and he did not return Edwards's calls to try and get an explanation. At last, Edwards received a message: Peter would be visiting London again and he would be staying at his usual hotel in Kensington. He would like to meet him. On the agreed morning, he went to meet him at his hotel. He was still very annoyed about all his wasted time and effort! But, as always, Peter was charming and had a ready explanation. "She tried to circumvent me," he said, meaning the female owner of the Italian company. "She made direct contact with the people I had developed as contacts in Brazil, when I had asked her not to do so. Some of them told me that this had happened. I think that she wanted to negotiate with them directly and cut me out of the agreed commission, that would have been payable to me for a successful sales contract."

Edwards was in a quandary; he had now known Peter for many years. Did he believe him or what he had been told by the Italian company's owner? In the end, he felt that he had to give Peter the benefit of the doubt and believe in his side of the story. "I am now part of a new business," said Peter. "It is in Tuscany and it is an established company making bio-degradable plastics. We are working closely with a brilliant Professor, at a nearby University, who is one of the world's greatest experts in this area. You must come out and see the factory, meet the people, and of course, the Professor. I will pay for your hotel and food if you can get yourself out there."

Edwards thought about this for a while and then he decided: he booked himself on to a budget flight to Pisa. Peter had booked him into a small hotel, in a charming spa town, in the Tuscan hills. He was not there to meet him when he landed, so Edwards had to take an expensive taxi from Pisa Airport to the hotel. The taxi fare took all the Euros that he had on him. Peter had promised to meet Edwards at the hotel the following morning and take him to the factory site, which was just off the main motorway, halfway between Pisa and Florence. In the morning, on cue, Peter picked him up in a brand new luxury Mercedes car. "This is part of my salary package with the company," he said.

They drove to the factory, a single storey building in an industrial estate, with some offices at one end. "Come in and meet everybody," said Peter, as he opened the door at the office end of the building. There were about a dozen people working there including a lady accountant, several female secretaries, an Italian marketing team of three men, and in the factory, where he was also shown around, at least four overall-clad workers operating an impressive amount of complex machinery.

4

"I must now introduce you to the most important person here," said Peter, taking Edwards to a glass box at the end of the factory section of the building. "This is Juliet, the daughter of our friend the Professor. She too is a Chemist, like her father, and he has lent her to us to help with developing new products." Edwards shook hands with a rather shy, very serious, bespectacled girl in her late twenties.

"Let us go to my office now," said Peter. "We can discuss strategy there and I will tell you about the role I see here for you."

They went back to the office section of the building. Through another door was a large Board Room with a long table and chairs. At the side of this room was another large table with about two hundred objects on it.

"What are all these?" asked Edwards, curiously.

"Those are all the products, made out of bio-degradable plastic, that we can make," replied Peter.

"But there are too many of them!" said Edwards.

"That is exactly what I want to discuss with you," said Peter. "We need a rational marketing and production strategy, now that I am in charge. Come into the Managing Director's office," he said, opening another door. "That's me!" he grinned.

They sat in Peter's impressive office and he told Edwards about the background to the company. "It was bought by an Englishman from an Italian some years ago," he said. "He lives in the North of England and made a lot of money working out in the Middle East. But buying this company was stupid; he does not speak Italian and hardly comes out here. Instead, he sends his son from time to time. He is a nice young man but knows nothing about business. You will meet him later. So I convinced the father to make me Managing Director and give me a good salary, plus some shares. But the company is running out of money fast as it has so few sales, so I have now convinced him to give me some more shares and I will bring in some more money to keep the company going." Peter grinned again. "I think that in say six months, I may be in a position to apply to the Italian Courts and take over the whole company. I have a cunning plan to do that!"

Edwards was surprised by what Peter had said. "But what do you want me to do?" he asked.

"You saw all the products on the table out there," said Peter. "This company has no marketing strategy. The Italian Marketing Director only looks after Italy, and he can speak only Italian. That is beside the fact that he is taking illegally a percentage back, for himself personally, on every sale. So, what I want you to do is to write me a paper on marketing strategy and identify the limited number of markets and products that we should concentrate on. Then you can help me to implement your plan."

"But will I be paid for this?" asked Edwards.

"Of course," said Peter. "You will be paid through a company, in London, which is owned by my girlfriend's mother. When you get back, I will arrange for you to visit their offices and agree your consultancy terms with them."

Edwards spent the rest of the day getting as much information as he could from the members of staff that could speak English, about the company, and the bio-degradable plastic products that they could make. He also sat with the company's lady accountant and discussed the financial situation of the company. They were soon to apply to the European Union for a cash grant, to expand their business and she was now getting that application ready to submit. That evening, he was introduced by Peter to the Professor, who had developed the bio-degradable plastics formula, and Peter bought them all a traditional Tuscan dinner at the hotel where Edwards was staying.

It was after that dinner, when the Professor had left and they were sitting in the hotel bar together, having a digestif, that Peter imparted some more information to Edwards. "I was in Sicily the other week," he said. "I met a man living here from Sicily and we flew together to that island. He introduced me there to the Head of the Mafia."

Edwards was amazed. "But what was it like?" he asked.

"Just like any other business meeting," replied Peter, but then he refused to say any more about what had been discussed.

Back in London, Edwards met the mother of Peter's English girlfriend, in her small office suite overlooking Westminster Abbey. The terms of Edwards's consultancy contract were agreed, printed out, and signed. Again Edwards would be paid a monthly retainer, starting immediately, over a period of six months, while he did his study, and he would then help to implement the new marketing strategy. The first monthly retainer arrived as Edwards began to put together the draft of the beginning of his marketing study. He was making good progress, by the time the second monthly payment was due and he had already sent the work he had completed to Peter, for his comments.

But the second monthly payment did not arrive. He queried the non-payment of his second retainer instalment with Peter, who referred him to the English company that had signed his contract. Edwards could get no answer from them. Several weeks went by, and he decided that he must stop work if he was not going to be paid. He informed Peter, who also seemed to ignore him. What was annoying was that he had heard from Peter that the Italian company had received the grant from the European Union. Eventually, he decided that he would have to make a formal legal claim for his money. He did so, and the curt reply he received from the mother of Peter's girlfriend was "That he could sue her company if he wanted to, but he would not get any money. She would just liquidate the company first!"

5

One of Edwards's friends, called Mike, had, some months before, expressed an interest in the Italian company. Edwards had given him Peter's contact details and Mike had driven all the way to Italy. He had visited Peter, met the company staff and was shown around the factory. He had spent a week in the rolling Tuscan hills, called at the company several more times and enjoyed his time off visiting a number of the local tourist sites and several vineyards. Edwards knew that Mike liked women; he collected "lady friends" whenever and wherever possible. When he got back, and Edwards met up with him again, it was clear that he had fallen into some kind of relationship with the company's lady accountant, who was an attractive widow.

From Mike, Edwards now began to receive regular updates on what had transpired at Peter's company, received by Mike, in reports from this lady accountant. The news was not good. Despite the grant that had been received from the European Union, and some grants and loans received from the local Italian Provincial Authority, the company had gone out of business. Edwards began to read articles on the Internet from the English-speaking Italian newspapers. From there, he read the news that the powerful Italian Financial Police had been called in to investigate, as a lot of money appeared to be missing from the company.

Peter was arrested and then had appeared in the local Court. He was charged that he had somehow misappropriated the money given by the European Union and by the local Italian authorities. He was allowed out on bail, but only if he stayed for most of his day in the house he had now rented, with his English girlfriend, who had now joined him, in the pleasant Tuscan spa town where Edwards had once stayed. But it appeared that the Financial Police could find little or no definite evidence against him so, eventually, he had to be released and he had then flown back to Malta.

A few months later, Mike had called Edwards. "My lady friend called me last week," he told him. "When her company folded up, she did not know what to do with all the company's financial records. So she took them home with her and stored them in her garage. She is now asking me what she should do with all these piles and piles of files?"

"She should take them to the Police immediately," replied Edwards. "No wonder that they could not find any proper evidence against Peter!"

So, it was arranged that the lady accountant contacted the local Police Station and the company's financial records were, at last, collected in a police van. "Hopefully they will provide the evidence against Peter that is needed," thought Edwards, who had now decided, after his two unfortunate experiences, to have nothing more to do with him.

6

But that was not the end of Peter's story. Mike had continued his search of the Internet and referred Edwards to several stories that had begun to be reported in the Maltese newspapers. Peter was now under suspicion of a number of major frauds. Over the years, he had persuaded a number of rich people to invest money in various schemes and the money had then seemed to disappear. To avoid arrest, he flew from Malta to London and began to stay at the large house owned by his English girlfriend's mother. It sat in the southern English countryside surrounded by a large estate.

In Malta, investigations were continuing. Edwards was now avidly following further reports in the Maltese newspapers. The total of the missing money was now reported to have reached seven and a half million Euros! One of the Maltese newspapers, somehow tracked down Peter, to the estate in the southern

English countryside, where he was staying. The Maltese authorities applied to the Maltese Courts and no fewer than seven European Arrest Warrants were issued, one for each count of suspected fraud that had now been entered against Peter. The Warrants were sent to England, where the London Metropolitan Police passed them to the local County Police Service in southern England, to execute.

One morning, the local Police arrived at the estate. "I am afraid that he is not here," Peter's English girlfriend told them. "He left early this morning and I do not know where he has gone." The Police left without even asking for permission to search the house.

The Maltese authorities were incensed, and the Maltese newspapers published articles about the inefficiency of the British Police. They demanded that something should be done. Eventually, the local County Police Service returned to the estate, but this time they were armed with a Search Warrant. They searched the house and found Peter, hiding under a bed. He was at last arrested, taken to London, and appeared before a Magistrates Court where his lawyer made clear that he would fight any extradition to Malta. The lawyer argued that his client was suffering from a serious disease, that needed to be treated in London, and produced a Medical Certificate to that effect.

He asked for Peter to be bailed and allowed to return to where he had been staying.

The matter was referred to a higher Court to decide, because of the amount of money that the Maltese government had said that was missing. This Court eventually decided to release Peter on bail, but under certain strict conditions, such as the surrender of his Passport and the need for him to report regularly to the local Police Station. Several people had to deposit large amounts of money, with the Court, as a Bail Security for him to be released.

There followed a prolonged Extradition Hearing, with his lawyers arguing that Peter was too ill to fly to Malta and that he could only obtain the medical treatment he needed in Britain. Further Medical Certificates were produced to this effect but, despite these, eventually the London Court decided that he was not ill enough not to be able to take the relatively short flight to Malta. Because of the amounts involved, the Maltese Courts would have to have the opportunity of trying him on the charges laid out in the seven European Arrest Warrants. At last, after all these delays, he was rearrested and, one morning, two Maltese Police Officers arrived at Heathrow Airport. Peter was handed over to them and he was bundled on to the aeroplane that was due to fly him back to Malta.

Before the Maltese Courts, the very next day, Peter was refused bail. The Maltese authorities were fully aware of how long and difficult it had been to extradite him from Britain, and they did not want him to leave Malta, by some means, again. There was now pressure on the Maltese government to get on with Peter's trail, and extract Justice, for the people that had lost large sums of money to Peter. Some were Maltese, but there were also some prominent Italians and a collection of other nationals. Nevertheless, the trial took its time; Justice in Malta seemed to move very slowly. All this time Peter was held in prison, and there were a series of complaints from his lawyers that his health was suffering and that his illness was getting worse, because of the prison conditions. He was moved to the Prison Hospital, but that did not seem to make his condition any better.

After about one year of Court proceedings, finally his lawyers got their way. A more sympathetic Judge agreed to release Peter on bail, just before Christmas, so that he could spend the time with his English girlfriend and the two children that she had now produced for him. The Court's conditions however were stringent; he had to surrender his Maltese Passport and report at 10 o'clock every morning to his local Police Station. He was not allowed out of the house he was staying in during the evening or overnight.

In London, Edwards picked up this news from articles in a number of Maltese newspapers, all of which had been following Peter's criminal trial very closely. Edwards had, at last, realised that Peter was just a fraudster and began to wish that he would be found guilty and spend many years in a Maltese prison. Then, perhaps, the Italian Financial Police would apply to have him extradited to Italy and he would then spend some more years in an Italian prison, for what he had done there.

But, after Peter's release on bail, there was a long silence. No more reports appeared in the Maltese press. Edwards had become so interested to find out what had happened that, after over twelve months of an absence of any more newspaper reports, he contacted several of the Maltese papers by email. He enquired from the individual reporters, that had been covering Peter's trial what, in the end, had happened with the case. But none of them replied. Edwards tried to think clearly. The trial had not seemed to have reached a conclusion as any verdict, be it guilty, or not guilty, would have been heavily publicised. If Peter had died from his illness, or had committed suicide, that, as well, would surely have been front-page news all over Malta. Only one other alternative seemed possible: Peter had escaped Justice!

Edwards had begun to surmise that, after reporting at the Police Station one morning, Peter had headed for the nearby island's airport. Edwards was sure that he must have a number of other Passports from different countries. Perhaps he had been helped to escape, by the organised crime connections in Sicily, that he had claimed to have had? A short flight from Malta to a European hub airport, and then an onward flight to Brazil, seemed the most possible scenario. Edwards knew that Peter still had many contacts in that country. But this final result, after such a long and expensive criminal case, would have been so embarrassing for the Maltese government, that they surely would have imposed some kind of news-blackout.

No Maltese newspaper would have dared to publicise this end to Peter's story. Only a few months before, a Maltese journalist had been killed by a bomb, placed under her car, for trying to investigate, too closely, Government corruption and its involvement with criminal activity. So, Edwards came to believe, that the "King of Italy", had somehow finally escaped his revolting Subjects. He had flown to a new country and a new life, where the opportunities for this illustrious person, would prove more fruitful, and his People more understanding and more loyal than his Subjects in Italy and Malta had ever proved to be!

But this, fortunately, was not the case, Peter had not escaped justice. It was just that the wheels of justice in Malta ground so very slowly! At last, Edwards found some later reports from a Maltese newspaper; Peter's Maltese lawyers had made every effort to delay justice, by a series of clever legal appeals, all of which then had to be heard. It was really ironic, that Peter had then appealed to the European Court of Human Rights that it was unjust for the Maltese Courts to take so long in judging him! The European Court found for him, but then awarded him a mere two thousand Euros for all his efforts! The cost of all this legal work must have been immense, and Edwards had to assume that it was all being paid for by Peter, desperate to avoid prison, from the money that he had stolen from others.

But, at last, some justice was achieved. Peter was found guilty on one of the fraud charges against him. Some twenty years before, he had stolen a relatively small amount of money from a famous Italian musician who had since passed away. For this crime, Peter was sentenced to two years in a Maltese jail. Edwards hoped that, not only was his prison cell very uncomfortable, but that he would then be found guilty of the other charges, and that his jail sentence would then be added to, in a series of long increments.

At the end of that long period in a Maltese jail, maybe, he could then be extradited to Italy, to face a further jail term for the frauds that he had carried out in that country. The "King of Italy" would be, at last, taken back to his own country, under escort, to face his Subjects and to account for the crimes that he had carried out in his Kingdom!

IRISH MIST

"Life is too short to read a bad book" – James Joyce

1

"Good Morning, sir. It's a Soft Morning," said the taxi driver, as Edwards opened the back door of his car. Edwards responded with a "Good Morning," and threw in his rather thick briefcase. It was made of heavy leather and he had bought it a few years before, for a cheap price, in a Bangkok street market. His previous very old briefcase had just fallen apart, as he was walking down a Bangkok street, from the weight of the too many papers that Edwards had put into it! His new briefcase served also as an overnight bag. It had a compartment for his papers, and a separate compartment that could hold his electric razor, his toilet bag, and several changes of shirts, socks, and underclothes. He got into the back seat of the taxi and gave the driver the address of the major aerospace and defence company that he was visiting that day.

As the car started off, Edwards smiled to himself. He had recognised the horse racing phrase that his taxi driver had used in greeting him. It described the condition of a racecourse that had been subjected to a period of light rain. Like many Irishmen, his driver must be a follower of the Sport of Kings! It was indeed a "Soft Morning"; the mist was descending vertically in a continuous and now heavy drizzle. They came out on to the main road, and ahead of them, Edwards could just discern the shrouded, great, white bulk of the Stormont building, on the top of its shallow hill. Completed in 1932, it housed the Northern Ireland Assembly, but this Assembly had now been suspended and the current direct rule, imposed from London since the restart of the current violence, was still in place.

Edwards's hotel had been carefully chosen; it was one of the few hotels in the city which were considered to be more secure, because of the constant Army and armed police patrols. The Irish Republican Army, known as the "I.R.A.", had broken their own earlier-declared temporary ceasefire, with a major bomb attack on Canary Wharf, the new financial centre for London. This bomb had killed two people, and caused an estimated £150 million of damage. It was just another incident in "The Troubles", as they were known, which had started again in 1972 after the day known as "Bloody Sunday", when fourteen Northern Ireland Catholics had been shot and killed by British troops.

Edwards now worked for a British Government department which helped British companies, large and small, export their goods and services overseas. He was appointed as a temporary senior Civil Servant and had been intensively vetted before being able to see classified material designated as above Secret. That morning he would be shown around the production facilities of the company he was visiting, including the line that produced military missiles. Then he would meet with their marketing teams to see if he could advise in any way about their international markets and the finance that might be available for their exports.

He had been given the required Security Briefing before leaving for Belfast. He had been told to never hire a taxi in the street, but to order one from the Help Desk at the Airport when he arrived, or from his hotel. They would know the safe Protestant taxi firms that could be used. There were Catholic taxi firms, but they were used only by the Catholics. If you took the wrong type of taxi, you might just never be seen again!

He had arrived in the late afternoon, the previous day, at Aldergrove Airport, which had been renamed as Belfast International Airport some ten years before. On the short British Airways flight from London, he had looked at the return ticket that had been booked for him. He did not fly back until an evening flight the next day. He decided that, when he arrived, he would ask to change his flight to an earlier departure, as he knew that he would be leaving his meeting tomorrow shortly after the in-house lunch that his hosts would give him. On landing, he had gone to the British Airways desk; a pretty girl sat behind it and Edwards asked her if he could change his ticket to an earlier return flight the next day?

She looked at him and said, "Wait a moment please, sir," in her strong Northern Irish brogue. She lifted a telephone and quietly spoke into it. Edwards waited.

"Can you come with me please, sir," said a male voice at his side. He turned; it was a British Army Corporal in full uniform. He was younger, taller, and fitter than Edwards and, at his hip, was a holstered handgun. Edwards decided quickly that he had better comply. He was led through a hidden door, down some stairs, along an underground corridor, and into a small room. Behind a desk sat an Army Sergeant Major, again, in full uniform. There was no chair for Edwards to sit on.

The soldier fixed Edwards with a stare. "You have asked to change you flight, sir?" he asked. Edwards confirmed that he had asked to do so. "I am sorry, sir," replied the Sergeant Major bluntly, "but you are not allowed to do so. We monitor you into here, and we monitor you out of here. Any changes to your flights, which we have been given the details of, are not allowed!"

Edwards accepted the inevitable and was shown back, by the Corporal, to the Airport's help desk, where he asked them to order him a taxi to the restaurant address that he had been given. In the taxi he reflected that this was a very different world from the mainland, and security was very tight, especially it seemed, for him. He soon arrived at the restaurant where he was to have dinner with representatives of the company that was hosting him, and which he was due to visit the next day. It seemed to be an excellent restaurant and he waited in the small bar for his hosts to arrive.

The first to arrive were two well dressed and rather beautiful ladies. They explained that their two male colleagues would shortly follow. They sat at a table in the bar together and drinks were ordered. Edwards's mood improved. They were very enjoyable company, and he found their Irish brogue most attractive to listen to. Rather unfortunately for Edwards, their two male colleagues soon arrived, and joined them for pre-dinner drinks. After about an hour they were all shown to their reserved table by the head waiter. Edwards immediately felt a little uncertain; it was a table right next to a large window overlooking the wide street, and he had been put to sit next to the window. After all, Edwards well knew that the I.R.A. had been making frequent bomb and shooting attacks for years in Belfast and in the rest of Northern Ireland.

"Are we ok here?" he found himself asking, rather nervously.

One of his male hosts answered him knowingly. "Don't worry," he said. "The I.R.A. do not come down this street!"

Edwards relaxed. In any conflict situation overseas, local knowledge was always very important. At last he felt that he could enjoy the charming female company again, and also his excellent gourmet dinner.

2

A decade earlier, Edwards had been working for a large international construction group. His job was to advise on all matters financial, and to try and find the finance for the group to carry out many of the projects which prospective clients wished to be built. He had made clear to all the marketing staff that he wanted to get involved at the earliest stage possible, in looking at prospective projects. It was a complete waste of time and money, if a lot of work was done on projects that needed to be financed, but really stood very little chance of raising the required loans to allow them to be constructed. He tried to establish close links with the various marketing departments and its personnel, so that his advice would always be asked at an early stage.

It was therefore a nice surprise, when a marketing representative of one of the more domestically orientated construction companies within the group, asked to see him. The man explained that, as well as the United Kingdom, he also looked after the Republic of Ireland. He had now gathered together a number of projects in Ireland which historically, before it was declared independent in 1922 as the Irish Free State, had been a part of Great Britain. He then asked Edwards if he would like to accompany him on a three-day trip to the Republic, visiting both Dublin and Cork, where he had identified a number of projects which would need finance for them to happen?

Edwards willingly accepted and a few weeks later they flew together, on an Aer Lingus flight, to Dublin. As their last meeting was to be in Cork, their return flight had been booked from Cork Airport back to London. They had passed a convivial, but hard working, two days in Dublin, staying at the prestigious Shelbourne Hotel. This hotel had been founded in 1824, when a native of County Tipperary, Martin Burke, had bought three large, adjoining, Georgian style town houses, overlooking St. Stephen's Green, a large landscaped public park in the centre of Dublin. He had joined them together and converted them into a much-needed luxury hotel.

Their days were spent in meetings but, on the second evening of their stay, after dinner, they had walked down to the bank of the River Liffey. There they had found a typical Irish public house and partook, of course, of the great Irish dark, dry, stout, first brewed by Arthur Guinness in his Dublin brewery in 1759. Edwards sipped his glass slowly, appreciating its full flavour. "I have drunk this before in London," he said to his colleague, "but I have never tasted anything like this. It is a completely different drink over here."

His colleague smiled. "They say that it is the water they use from the River Liffey to brew it, that gives it that great taste!" he replied.

The entrance door to the street opened, and in came a rather scruffy old man, in a torn and rather dirty raincoat. He did not appear to have shaved for several days. He was carrying a violin case. He went to the bar, took off his raincoat and sat down on a bar stool. Underneath his coat, he had on a creased and rather worn suit. He took a fiddle out of his case and started to play. He played beautifully, a whole series of traditional Irish songs and dances. Soon the whole hostelry was singing and dancing to his merry tunes!

The next morning, Edwards found that he was suffering from a headache, which did not seem to go away. Normally he would have partaken of the excellent full breakfast provided by the Shelbourne Hotel. But it had to be an early, quick, light Continental breakfast on that day, as they were leaving on an early morning train for Cork. In the early evening they were due to fly back direct from Cork Airport to London. They took a taxi to Dublin's Connolly Station, and Edwards's colleague approached the ticket office to buy their tickets. Edwards was just behind him, so he heard the conversation with the ticket clerk.

"Two Single First Class tickets to Cork, please," said Edwards's colleague in a very clear voice.

"Oh sir, will that be Return tickets?" came back the reply.

Edwards's colleague repeated his request for "Two Single First Class tickets to Cork, please."

A look of horror came over the ticket clerk's face. "Oh sir, does that mean that you won't be coming back?"

Eventually, the tickets were successfully purchased and they found their way to the train to Cork. They sat on their single seats opposite each other, with a table between them. No sooner had they left Dublin that it was announced, on the public address system, that a complementary full Irish Breakfast would now be served to all First Class passengers, and that other passengers could purchase this too, if they wished. Edwards's colleague looked at him. "Can you manage two breakfasts?" he asked.

"After last night, I can manage anything!" replied Edwards.

The full Irish Breakfast was served at their table; tasty Irish bacon and sausages, a cooked tomato and mushrooms, a fried egg, and a piece of fried bread! To go with it, an ample supply of toast with Irish butter and Scottish marmalade, was provided. All this was washed down with a glass of orange juice and as many refills of their coffee cups, that they needed. They moved, at no great speed, in a generally south-western direction. As he ate his most welcome second breakfast, Edwards looked out of the window. A journey like this often provoked a feeling of nostalgia within him.

He loved train travel. It went back to his childhood days, when he used to travel, quite often, from his home in Shropshire to his grandmother's house, overlooking the sea, on the beautiful island of Anglesey in North Wales. The sight, sound, and smell of the great steam engine that always pulled The Irish Mail express train, came back to him. The line through Anglesey ended at Holyhead, the main port to take the ferry boats to Ireland. His mind went back to his first visit to Ireland. On one holiday, when he was still a small boy of about six years old, he and his parents had not got off the train at the last stop before Holyhead, as they normally did, to take the local taxi to his grandmother's house. Instead, they continued on to Holyhead and took the ferry for Ireland.

It had been exciting for the boy to board the great ship, but it proved to be a stormy crossing of the Irish Sea. Edwards remembered that he and his mother had fared well, but his father had suffered horribly from sea sickness. When they landed at the port of Dun Laoghaire, they took the short train journey to Dublin to change trains. Then there was a long, slow, wet and windy onward train journey to Sligo, in the extreme north-western corner of Ireland. There they had been met by the husband of his mother's cousin, who took them to stay with them in Ballyshannon, where they lived overlooking the wild Atlantic coast. He was an engineer and he was helping to build the new nearby hydro-electric project.

The very young Edwards had been struck by the rugged countryside, the lack of human habitation, and the wet and windy weather in this remote outpost. That kind of weather had continued for their whole week's stay. It had seemed, to the young boy, to be so different, and so very far away from his home in a small town in Shropshire.

But today was a dry and sunny morning. Ireland was indeed the beautiful "Emerald Isle," that it was romantically named. With its average heavy rainfall, the fields had just that deep green colour. Everywhere there were herds of contented cows and little villages, with the expected prominent Catholic Church. They stopped at three or four railway stations in small towns, and then it was announced that their next stop would be Limerick Junction.

Edwards smiled to himself. He remembered the Director that he had to report to when he had first joined a merchant bank in the City of London. He was a charming man, and he bore the Irish title that gave him a seat in the House of Lords. He was from these parts, and his ancestors owned a castle outside the town. Edwards had heard him give a speech at a number of formal dinners and charmingly, he had always finished off each speech with an Irish limerick, a humorous five line poem, that he had composed himself especially for the occasion.

They stopped at Limerick Junction, and an announcement came over the public address system: "This train is now an Express Train to Cork. Which means, that this train will not be stopping at the stations between here and Cork. Which means, that Cork will be the next stop!"

The other occupants of the carriage really could not understand why Edwards and his colleague fell about laughing. His colleague, who had travelled to Ireland many time before, spluttered out, between his laughter, in a mock Irish accent "To be sure. To be sure. To be sure. That's the Irish way!" This only served to renew Edwards's laughter.

They arrived at Cork and took a taxi to the impressive City Hall. There they were received by the Lord Mayor of Cork and several of his Councillors, who wanted to discuss a major rejuvenation of the city's dock area on the River Lee. The Lord Mayor greeted Edwards most warmly; "We are so sorry about the Troubles up north!" was the first thing that he said.

3

Edwards was attending a marketing meeting at the Ministry of Defence. He had entered that great white bulk of a building on Whitehall through its eastern entrance, showing his Security Pass and then entering one of the circular hard plastic tubes, whose outer door then closed on you, sealing you in. Not only then did it seem to weigh you, but it was said to have sensors inside which could detect metal objects or explosives. Only when "The Tube" was fully satisfied, did its inner door open and release you into the building!

Edwards was now an adviser to government on the provision of finance for certain British exports. The meeting was held in a secure room, which had been "swept" for any listening devices. It was to discuss a long list of numerous international sales opportunities for British defence manufacturers, to sell their products overseas. Edwards's job was to comment on those that would probably require finance in order to complete the sale. At the end, a small number of export opportunities for second-hand equipment sales from the stocks of the British Armed Forces, were discussed. Edwards woke up, when he heard the name of a particular country in the Middle East, in regard to a potential, major sale.

"I expect that they will need finance, to be able to do that particular deal," he said. Then he added, "Of course, we cannot offer the usual type of Government Export Credit support, since the equipment is currently owned by the British Government. But there may be a way that we can get over that problem. I will think about it."

The senior Civil Servant chairing the meeting looked at him. "I would be grateful if you would please," he said. "But there is another problem. We do not believe that the Minister of Defence in that country is particularly pro-British. We think that maybe the French have got to him. Therefore, we have somehow to get a personal message through to the Ruler himself, about how attractive this deal might be to them."

Edwards's colleague, that he knew well, then intervened. "That Minister went to the Sorbonne and we think that French Intelligence has a record of some of his student misdeeds there," he said. "No doubt the French will use that if they want to! They would like to sell this equipment to them, as new equipment and, no doubt, some money will then go into private pockets to complete the deal. It could be very much a "carrot and stick" situation."

Edwards knew that this colleague was a senior intelligence officer, so he probably knew what he was talking about. "But, of course, the Ruler finished his education here, and then went on to Sandhurst for his army officer training. So he has always been rather pro-British," Edwards countered. "Let me think about it and let you know," repeated Edwards.

So he did think about it; he recalled how over ten years before, he was working with a merchant bank to put together and finance a major construction project in the same Middle Eastern country. Then, suddenly, an idea came to him. He picked up his office telephone and dialled the number of the same bank. He asked the telephonist, who answered his call, to speak to a particular employee. She replied that he no longer worked there. Edwards then asked for another senior employee that he knew was still with the bank. His secretary answered and Edwards asked for him.

"What was it about?" asked the Secretary.

"I am afraid that I cannot tell you," said Edwards. "But if you give him my name, if he is there, he will take my call."

He was there in his office, and they chatted for some ten minutes to catch up on each other's lives. Only then, did Edwards ask his question. "Has Paul left the bank?" he asked.

"No, Paul is now Managing Director of our subsidiary bank in Dublin," came the reply.

At the next marketing meeting, in the Ministry of Defence, Edwards waited until the end to bring up his suggestion. "I have been thinking about the sale of that major amount of British owned equipment to the Middle East," he said, and named the country. "I have now thought of a way that we can structure the finance. I also have a banking contact, from many years back, who can put that finance together and through his wife, can pass a private message to the Ruler."

"How is that possible?" asked the meeting's chairman.

Edwards replied carefully. "He is married to a very senior lady from that country, whose family is thought to be even older and with more status, than the Ruling Family. The Ruler will take her call if she calls him on a private basis."

The chairman looked impressed and consulted his colleagues around the table. They all agreed that Edwards should try his suggested route. "You realise that this must be done in great secrecy," added the chairman.

"Yes, of course," replied Edwards. "But my man now lives and works in Dublin for the same bank. I will have to go over there for the day to meet him. Of course, I do not know if he and his wife will be prepared to help us."

The chairman rather grudgingly agreed to Edwards's day trip. "But be very careful," he said. "We do not want the Irish government to find out that we are setting up an officially-backed overseas defence sale on their territory. Of course, if they find out, they may just tell the French as well. Make sure that you inform our Embassy there first, before your trip," he added.

Edwards knew that a typical British Embassy often seemed to leak such information. "I think that if I do that, it will not remain a secret mission for very long," he replied. He was determined not to inform the Embassy of his trip before, or after, his visit!

Edwards obtained the telephone number and address of their subsidiary bank in Dublin, from its London parent company. Then he rang up Paul, who was surprised to hear from him, after all these years. "You know what I do now?" asked Edwards. Paul replied that he had heard from his London colleagues, about what was Edwards's current role.

"I need to meet you to discuss something," said Edwards. "I will fly over for the day."

"I will be very happy to meet you again, and I will certainly buy you a good lunch," said Paul, remembering how, as one of Edwards's friends had once kindly put it, that "Edwards was a legend in his own lunchtime!"

Edwards knew that somehow, he had to let Paul know the clandestine nature of their proposed meeting, so he chose his next words very carefully. "It is strictly confidential and sensitive," he said hoping that these words would help Paul to understand.

Paul seemed to do so. They then fixed a date for Edwards's visit to Dublin, and a time that they would meet. Then Paul gave Edwards the reassurance that he needed. "Have you got a mobile phone?" he asked. Edwards told him that he had this piece of new technology, supplied free of charge by his employer. "When you get to my office, call me from just outside it," said Paul. "I will come out and meet you, and we will then go somewhere for a quiet lunch together!"

Edwards realised that Paul was worried about the integrity of his office; had someone perhaps planted some listening devices inside it? At least Paul seemed to be aware of the difficulties of keeping these kind of things totally confidential, indeed, Secret.

4

It was not until his British Airways flight had levelled out at its cruising altitude, that Edwards began to think about a Cover Story. If he was asked by the Irish Immigration authorities, at Dublin Airport, why he was coming to Ireland for just a day, what would he say? He knew that every Cover Story should have as much truth in it as possible, in order to be plausible. He decided, in the end, to say that he was a businessman, who was flying over to meet an old friend, who now worked in Dublin in the financial sector. "He wanted to hear about the successful growth of the financial sector in Dublin, over the last few years. He thought that he knew some people in London, who could be interested in investing in the property sector in the city."

But he need not have bothered as when, after the short flight, he had to present himself to the young Irish Immigration official at his desk. The man had merely looked at the front of Edwards's British Passport, and then waved him through. Without the Irish authorities demanding a list of all their passengers from British Airways, thought Edwards, they would not even know that I have been here! Edwards had already studied a map of Dublin and identified where Paul's office was located. Outside the terminal building, it was a warm and sunny day. He took the first taxi from the long rank of waiting vehicles. He told the driver to drop him, not at Paul's office address, but in an adjoining street, so that he could walk to it. Edwards was being careful not to leave any obvious trail!

He quickly found the street where Paul's office was and established which side of the street had even numbers; the address of Paul's office was an even number. He crossed the street in order to be on the odd number side, and stopped occasionally to look into a shop window. He always then glanced quickly behind him, and also in front of him, to try and see if anybody was following him. He was soon directly opposite Paul's office building. He was five minutes early; they had agreed to meet at midday. He went down the street a little further, then took out his mobile telephone in order to call Paul.

"I am just opposite your office," he told him.

"Look to your left," replied Paul. "On my side of the street you will see a coffee bar about four buildings down. Go into it and order yourself a coffee. I will join you in about a quarter of an hour."

Edwards was wondering if Paul had gone to a window, identified Edwards, and was watching him to see if he could spot anyone who might be following him. Edwards crossed the street again, went into the coffee bar, which was almost empty, and bought a Café Latte at the counter. He then took it and sat down at a small table in the corner, but facing the door. He was out of sight from anyone else in the coffee bar. Edwards took out his mobile telephone and under the edge of the table, so that nobody could see what he was doing, he removed the battery from his mobile. Fortunately this mobile telephone was made, so that you could just press a simple catch and the battery would come away.

The mobile telephone is an excellent modern surveillance device. The intelligence organisations of many countries now have the technology, not only to listen to mobile calls that were made, but also to switch on the microphone of the telephone, to be able to listen to any conversations that were happening face to face. Even if the telephone was turned off, this advanced technology could turn the device back on again to listen to what was being said, and the telephone's owner would never be any the wiser. But, without any power from the battery, this could not happen.

While doing his government advisory work, Edwards often had to give up his mobile telephone, against a numbered receipt, if he was attending a particularly sensitive meeting. All the telephones from every participant in the meeting, including his, were then put into a sound proof box, outside the room in which the meeting was happening and were collected back after the meeting had finished. So Edwards well understood the risks of modern technology; he carefully put his mobile telephone back into one of his pockets, and its battery into another.

Edwards had just finished his coffee when Paul entered. He spotted Edwards immediately, and Edwards rose to shake hands with him. "Just follow me," said Paul. He led Edwards to the side of the counter, down a short passageway, past the toilets, and then through the door marked Fire Exit at the end. Edwards found himself in a narrow alleyway. Paul looked carefully both ways, then soundlessly closed the door behind them, turned left, and followed by Edwards, walked quickly towards the end of the alleyway. Edwards was impressed, it was a perfect "walk through." Anyone watching the front of the coffee bar, would probably not know about this back exit, and would think that both men were still inside. He realised that somehow Paul knew about basic counter-surveillance techniques.

"Have you got a mobile telephone with you?" Edwards asked Paul, just to make sure.

He was relieved when Paul replied "No. I did not want us to be disturbed, so I left it in my office!"

They soon emerged into an adjoining street that ran at right-angles, to the street where Paul's office was located. Paul checked behind him and in front of him, and then hailed a taxi. He gave the driver the name of another street and they both got into the vehicle. They then both seemed to relax a little. They chatted together about old times, and colleagues which they had both known some ten years before. The taxi soon arrived at its destination, they got out, and Paul paid off the driver.

"It is just a short walk from here," he said. "It is not an expensive restaurant, but it has good food. I have not booked a table but, at this time of the day, we should get one, if we are quick."

They walked briskly and arrived at the restaurant, which was on the bank of the River Liffey. It was a modern building, and it had large picture windows, with an excellent view of the river. It was already partly full. Paul asked for a table for the two of them, but then, as the waitress was leading them to a corner table, asked if they could sit at a small table in the middle of the room. They continued their conversation about the past, as they ordered their food and drinks. Very quickly, the restaurant seemed to fill up. Edwards looked around approvingly. It now seemed to be full of young, pretty Irish girls. There were a few young men too, on their lunchbreak, and the noise volume in the restaurant had now increased almost to a crescendo, as they all chatted loudly to each other.

Edwards smiled approvingly at Paul; it would be almost impossible for anyone else to hear what they were saying to each other, even if there was a microphone under their table! Paul had selected the restaurant, had made no booking, and had even selected the table they now sat at. The Irish authorities would have had to put a microphone, under every table, in every restaurant in Dublin, to be sure of catching their conversation. When their first course arrived of Dublin Bay prawns, accompanied by a good white wine, chosen by Paul, Edwards judged that the time was right to get down to business.

"You know what I do now?" he said quietly. Paul leaned forward to listen to him carefully. "There is a major defence opportunity in a country that you know well and from where, I remember, that your wife comes from."

Paul just nodded. "There is a problem," continued Edwards. "We believe that their Minister of Defence may be against the deal, so we need your lady wife to get a personal message to the Ruler. Would that be possible please?"

Paul grinned and replied. "You know that they used to play together as young children? They speak frequently together, on the telephone, in their local Arab dialect of course. I will ask her tonight, but I am sure that she will not mind doing this. She now looks at Britain as her home."

Edwards was overjoyed and proceeded to tell Paul, very carefully, what his wife should say. Then he described the military equipment, which the Ministry of Defence wanted to sell to this Middle East country. Paul took a blank piece of paper and a pen out of his jacket, and proceeded to make some notes.

"Don't worry," he said. "My writing is terrible and nobody else will be able to read it. Once the call is finished, I will burn this piece of paper."

"But you are doing us a great favour," said Edwards. "It is only right that we should do one back." He then explained the need for finance for this deal and how he thought that it could be structured. "This is something that you can take to your colleagues in London," he concluded.

"Of course," said Paul. "Thank you for that. I will make sure that I contact only those colleagues that I think are secure. In fact, I will write to one of them that I know well. Nobody stops and opens letters very often, these days, to read them. But, I will leave certain vital information out, just in case. If there is a positive response from London, I will fly over there to help set the financing deal up face-to-face. I am sure that they will then pay for me to go to my wife's country, and there I can meet people that I have known for years. That will help to make the finance happen at that end."

Edwards was very happy with this result; he thanked Paul profusely, and for the rest of their excellent lunch, they chatted about other things. Then they took two separate taxis: Paul went back to his office, and Edwards went out to Dublin airport. Edwards flew back in the late afternoon to London, well satisfied with his day trip to Dublin.

The telephone call was made by Paul's wife and a full commitment to buy the British equipment, from the very top, was soon received. Nobody could contest this decision, once the Ruler had made it.

A few weeks later, the British Ambassador was called in, by the Ruler himself, to express his delight at this excellent deal that he had been offered. Fortunately, the British Ambassador had been briefed, with a Top Secret encrypted message marked "For Your Eyes Only", just the previous day. Otherwise he would not have known what the Ruler was talking about and what to say to him in reply. The reply that he did make confirmed, of course, that this deal could now take place, and that the finance to enable it to happen had already been made available!

ACKNOWLEDGEMENTS

It is now customary at the end of a volume such as this, to write some Acknowledgements to the people who have helped you in composing, writing, or checking your writing efforts. Unfortunately, because of my advanced years, some of those have already passed on in front of me. But I should nevertheless acknowledge them and state that they are all still strong in my memories.

Thomas Marshall RN was my maternal grandmother's lover; she left my mother's father to live with him. He contributed the true account of the first Battle of the Falkland Islands contained within this volume. Through his wonderful stories of life in the Royal Navy, when it was the largest Navy on Earth, he inspired me as a young boy with the wanderlust for travel. My dear mother contributed the story of how her honeymoon, in the South of France in 1934, was rudely interrupted by the arrival of a letter from her own mother.

My late, dear friend MC told me the fascinating story of his life, which I then turned into one of my stories. His life story seemed to me to be a little far-fetched, so I checked it out with my very good friend JB, who now resides in New York. He had, by then, confided in me what I had suspected for some time, that he had been a long-standing, senior American intelligence agent. He had, years before, introduced MC to me and he now confirmed to me, that the story that MC had given to me, was substantially true. My grateful thanks to JB, for his introduction to MC, and also for the introduction of several more of his well-placed contacts, from around the world.

I must also pay tribute to the help and interest of my numerous friends; I have often distributed my raw stories to them, and have always received back their encouragement. I should also acknowledge the unconscious contribution made to my stories by some of my friends and former colleagues who, by their past actions and thoughts, have certainly helped me to write them.

A special contribution has been made by my good friend Rob Green, who has used his skills and brilliance to produce a series of videoed interviews with me, based upon my stories, my past life, and present thoughts. His hard work on this series of interviews can now be found on YouTube, so that those who wish, can watch me "live." I thank him for all his efforts and also for expertly proofreading this book. You can find the first in the series by searching YouTube for "@englishmanasks – Christopher Spencer." If that is not successful, submit the same search to Google.

ACKNOWLEDGEMENTS

Finally, I should thank my readers and I hope that they will enjoy this effort to gather together some of my Shorter True Stories, as I call them. My stories are meant to entertain and indeed educate; they are all true and really happened to me! There are more to come, as I have already written even more true stories, and I am still writing. So I hope, if fate will allow me, to bring out a further third volume before my inevitable demise. By this means, I hope to pass on my knowledge and my unique life experience to others, and to the next generations, to inspire those that follow, I hope, to always seek Reality and the Truth!

Christopher Spencer.
May, 2023.

Milton Keynes UK
Ingram Content Group UK Ltd.
UKHW010625121023
430452UK00001B/7

9 781805 413059